# SUSSEX WARTIME RELICS AND MEMORIALS

## WRECKS, RELICS & MEMORIALS FROM SUSSEX AT WAR 1939-1945

MARTIN F. MACE

HISTORIC MILITARY PRESS

*By the same author and published by the Historic Military Press:*

'Frontline Sussex - The Defence Lines of West Sussex 1939-1945'.
ISBN 1 901313 00 X.
An illustrated guide to the pillboxes and associated defences built in West Sussex during the Second World War, containing a comprehensive list of over 120 sites of such structures that can still be found today.

# SUSSEX WARTIME
# RELICS AND MEMORIALS

Published 1997 by the Historic Military Press,
Green Arbor, Rectory Road, Storrington, West Sussex, RH20 4ES.

ISBN 1 901313 01 8.

HISTORIC MILITARY PRESS

Printed in the United Kingdom by BDA Associates, Unit T,
Rich Industrial Estate, Avis Way, Newhaven, East Sussex, BN9 0DJ.
01273-516566.

*Front Cover: A 12-pounder artillery emplacement on the cliff top at Newhaven Fort, Newhaven, East Sussex.*

*Back Cover: The remains of a Mark II Churchill Tank, near the South Downs Way above Storrington, West Sussex.*

# CONTENTS

*Above: One of the few wartime defences still in the ownership of the Ministry of Defence. This anti-infantry pillbox can be seen at the military base at Thorney Island, SU 767011.*

# INTRODUCTION

It was the early hours of the 13th June 1944, D-Day was seven days old, and so far the shift had been peaceful. Perched on top of the Martello Tower in Dymchurch, Kent, were Mr E.E. Woodland and Mr A.M. Wraight, their uniforms carrying the badge of the 'Royal Observer Corps'. The first track had only been moments before, the second was as much a shock as the first.

As with the first track, the second was an extraordinary apparition - a long rocket shape, spewing sparks and flames from its rear, and it passed making a noise akin to a "Model-T Ford going up a hill!". The apparition's bearing was checked, and for only the second time ever in the United Kingdom, the words "Mike Two, Diver - Diver - Diver" were shouted into the telephone. This message arrived at the Royal Observer Corps Centre at Maidstone, where the receiving controller was still recovering from the shock of the first track, before being passed onto the underground bunker at Bentley Priory , the nerve centre of our wartime air defence. Here all thoughts of a warm bed and sleep were erased - Nazi Germany had just unleashed its latest weapon on Britain - the V1.

The first V1 had been tracked as far as Gravesend where, 9 minutes after being seen by Dymchurch, it crashed causing a large explosion. The second, reported at 04.15, had altered its course and was now headed for Sussex!. As it flew along, at a pace not seen before, its track was followed by the various Royal Observer Posts, who in turn reported it to their control room at Horsham, and the radar stations at Pevensey, Truleigh Hill and Poling. Air raid sirens began to wail - people took to the shelters and anti-aircraft gun crews ran to their weapons. Messages flashed from Bentley Priory back into Sussex - alerting the RAF Stations and Military bases. All the while, the V1 had continued on, eventually falling to earth and exploding near the London to Brighton Railway line north of Cuckfield. This, only the second V1 to ever fall on Britain, was to be one of many!.

From this little story, one can see how much was involved in the tracking of one single rocket - radar stations, Observer Corps Posts, Control Rooms and so on - the list is endless. What is more surprising is the number of such wartime features that still remain here in Sussex - not only those involved in air defence, but from all areas of the defence of this country and its people.

This book is intended to provide the reader with an insight into what may be found lurking in the corner of a local field or hidden by a seemingly innocent clump of trees. It is by no means a definitive list, but sets out to provide as wide a selection of these wartime wrecks, relics and memorials as possible. Some of the sites are well known and others are documented in other books. Equally, there have been publications along similar lines published before, but none I hope with such a wide variety of sites as in the forthcoming pages.

Many of the sites are readily accessible, located on public footpaths or common land, whilst others are within private property - in all cases a grid reference and brief directions are supplied. A few are located within museums or public attractions. The two most obvious examples here are the Military Aviation Museum at Tangmere (Pickett-Hamilton Fort) and Newhaven Fort. The latter is a haven of military architecture, with gun batteries and emplacements of various ages perched on the cliffs above the Port of Newhaven. This diversity will be noticed in the following pages as Newhaven and its environs will reoccur time and again, and for that reason sites such as Fort Newhaven will be well worth a visit to many readers.

Despite over fifty years having passed since the end of the war, one of the most common elements of modern warfare, explosives, can still be found in often surprising quantities. An obvious danger exists with such articles - a danger best dealt with by professionals. The recovery of the Churchill Tank produced a number of unexploded rounds as well as remains of PIAT anti-tank shells; the Hurricane crash site also unearthed .303 bullets; whilst a simple walk across the South Downs at Amberley led to the discovery of a field littered with exploded and unexploded mortar bombs!. Exploring any military site carries with it a risk - so please take care!.

Martin F. Mace,
Steyning, September 1997.

# MERSTON
## AIRFIELD BATTLE COMMAND CENTRE

*Location: On private agricultural land, Marsh Farm, north of Marsh Lane.*
*Map reference: SU 891027.*

*Right: Poking out of the ground on the southern perimeter of the wartime airfield at Merston is the Observation Post of the airfields wartime Battle Control Centre. Clearly visible here is the steel reinforced slit through which the Local Defence Officer would monitor the situation on the ground. This slit gives a 360 degree field of vision, allowing a complete view of the whole airfield.*

Bombs exploding within the airfield perimeter; the control tower destroyed and on fire, Luftwaffe fighters strafing the runway and reports of German Paratroopers in the village 2 miles away!...... The Airfield's Commanding Officer, the Local Defence Officer, important signalmen, amongst others, all withdraw to the safety of the Battle Control Centre. Its purpose was, as its name suggests, to house the staff needed to co-ordinate the airfields defence in times of attack. Thankfully, apart from exercises, this example on the wartime airfield at Merston was never used in anger. Wartime Control Centres were built from one of two designs, and this example at Merston, built from the Air Ministry design drawings 11008/41, is the more common example.

*Above: This is the main passageway, (marked 'E' opposite), facing from the direction of the main entrance steps towards the chemical closet. The first door on the left is the entrance into the messengers and runners quarters, 'C'.    Below: This picture shows a flooded general office - note the tide marks on the wall!. It is in here that the Station C/O might well have gathered his staff. This photo was taken from the steps below the escape hatch, 'G', and shows the remains of the original lighting system still bolted to the re-inforced concrete roof.*

Normally, the only part of the Battle Control Centre that would have been visible above ground level would have been the Observation Post. The example here at Merston is however quite prominent and has been built only semi-sunken. This is a response to the high water table in the area and is done to prevent flooding. The building now has about 2 foot of water above its floor, but this is probably due to fifty years of rainfall entering via the escape hatch and main stairway.

The 11008/41 design of Battle Control Centre was introduced by the Air Ministry to be built at those airfields where the Local Defence Authority could find no other building that maybe adapted for the task. The design itself consists of a complex of five underground rooms with walls built from reinforced concrete some 13.5 inches thick.

The most important part of the structure was the observation post. Here the floor was built some 3ft higher than the other rooms so enabling a clear, unobstructed 360' view of the airfield. The cupola itself was 6ft square and capped with an enormously thick layer of re-inforced concrete. From this room, the unfolding battle would be observed, with the Local Defence Officer passing his instructions to his staff in the adjacent rooms, who in turn distributed the orders to the relevant defence positions in and around the airfield.

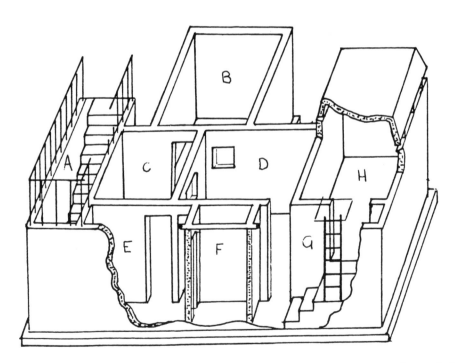

*Above: A diagrammatic representation of the Merston Battle Control Centre. A: Entry Stairs; B: Rest room and sleeping quarters; C: Messengers and runners quarters; D: General Office; E: Passage; F: Chemical closet; G: Escape Hatch; H: Observation post. (Reproduced by kind permission of the FlyPast Magazine).*

*Above: This general view of the Battle Control Centre shows how far raised above ground level the actual structure is. On the left is the Observation Post, (marked H overpage), whilst in the middle is the roof of the rest room and sleeping quarters (B). On the right are the entrance steps - here protected by concrete blast walls and not metal railings as on the diagram. Below: Only a few feet behind the control centre can be found some of the other airfield remains, in this case some of the perimeter track.*

# NEWHAVEN
## 12-POUNDER COASTAL BATTERY

*Access: By foot through the grounds of Newhaven Fort, Fort Road.*
*Map reference: TQ 448009.*

As you read through this book you will come to see that the Fort at Newhaven contains a variety of wartime structures - one of which is the 12-pounder gun emplacement located on the cliff top overlooking the harbour. In fact two 12-pounder emplacements were constructed during World War Two, each containing a single quick-firing 12 pounder gun.

The structure of the emplacement is simple. The gun floor is constructed from concrete and below which are located the lockers for storage of ammunition. A brick wall is built round the rear of the emplacement, and a solid concrete roof protrudes out over the gun floor. These serve to protect the gun crews from both the elements and being strafed by enemy aircraft. The entrance and exit steps lead from the rear of the emplacement through an arch way alongside the ammunition lockers.

Such 12 pounder emplacements were constructed along the length of the Sussex coastline, though almost all have since been removed. Worthing, for example, is believed to have had at least 6 of these 12-pounder emplacements protecting its beaches. One other survivor can be found on a small hill alongside the coast road at Pett Level, east of Hastings (see page 75).

*Right: Entry to the gun floor is achieved via these steps from the main area of the fort. They have a distinctly 'pre-war' feel, suggesting that the wartime builders of this gun post had decided to make use of an existing site.*

*Below: Beyond the 12-pounder gun can be seen the harbour mouth itself. This is the very reason for the gun being placed here - to prevent attack on the harbour by fast moving enemy boats. Had an attack been made, searchlights would have attempted to illuminate the enemy boat, allowing the gun crews a better chance of hitting the target!.*

# BROADBRIDGE HEATH
## ANTI-TANK BARRIER

> Access: By foot along public footpath from the end of Wickhurst Lane.
> Map reference: TQ 145304.

*Right: Following the public footpath from the end of Wickhurst Lane in Broadbridge Heath will bring you to Mill Bridge. Here can be seen two examples of the large road barriers constructed on bridges in Sussex. The one shown on the right has been tipped over, possibly to allow better access across the bridge, and its foundations can clearly be seen. Also visible is the large slot on the top, which would have held the barrier in place - often a piece of railway track. The block on the other side of the bridge is still in place, and has not been moved, thus allowing it to become overgrown!.*

During the Second World War , almost all river crossings in Sussex became defended points. In fact rivers such as the Arun, Adur and Ouse became what is now known as 'Stop Lines'. Along these rivers the banks were fortified and river crossings defended by the use of mines, pillboxes, flame defences and anti-tank blocks, amongst others.

These anti-tank tank blocks were intended to prevent vehicular passage, and whilst the tank or vehicle was held up trying to cross, it would have come under fire from the defenders in their pillboxes and trenches. Similar anti-tank barriers can be seen in many locations throughout Sussex, including:

Morgans Green. The bridge over River Arun at Gibbons Mill, TQ 073307.

Handcross. 14 of these blocks straddles the A279 at Warren Wood, TQ 246290.

Scaynes Hill. Covering the bridge over the river Ouse, Freshfield Mill, TQ 385245.

# HAYWARDS HEATH
## HOME GUARD GRAVE

> Access: By foot in grounds of Haywards Heath Cemetery, North Road.
> Map reference: TQ 342238.

*Left: Plot C.G., Grave 136, of the Cuckfield (Haywards Heath) Cemetery. Located on the north side of the cemetery is this Commonwealth War Graves Commission Grave Stone to Volunteer Gilbert Kent. Kent was a member of the 13th Sussex (Haywards Heath) Battalion of the Home Guard. He died, aged 62, on the 1st June 1941. The reason for his death is not recorded, but could have been the result of an air raid or sudden illness whilst on duty. He was the son of Edward James Kent and Susanah Kent, who also lived in Haywards Heath, and died leaving a wife, Ellen Kent.*

It is sad to note that all cemeteries and churchyards, almost without exception, contain the graves of those members of the armed services killed in action, and that these graves are cared for by the Commonwealth War Graves Commission. It is, however, unusual to find a grave for a member of the Home Guard. This is explained by the fact that the commemoration of the dead of certain auxiliary and civilian organisations, who while not members of the armed forces, but were involved to some degree with the armed forces or in war work, is the responsibility of the Commission. The Commission therefore cares for the graves of members of the Home Guard, where their death occurred whilst officially on duty and if this is confirmed by the Ministry Of Defence.

Access: By foot along public footpath from Exceat Car Park, A259.
Map reference: TV 522976.

*Right: Had any German troops ever landed on the beaches at Cuckmere Haven they would have come under withering fire from the machine guns placed inside this structure. Equally the thick concrete walls would have meant that the attackers would have found it very hard indeed to silence the guns. The American made 0.5 inch Browning heavy machine gun would have the most likely occupant of this pillbox, but failing that use would have been made of other weapons, such as the British made Bren Gun.*

At an early stage in the war British Military Intelligence was led to believe that a German Invasion of Britain would involve troops landing in several places on the south coast - including at Cuckmere Haven, east of Seaford. It is here that the River Ouse emerges into the English Channel, having cut a deep valley through the South Downs - thereby creating a natural route north through the Downs. As a result the beaches, valley floor and hillsides at Cuckmere Haven were transformed into a vast defensive area. On the west side of the river is a large anti-tank wall, whilst on the eastern side can be found pillboxes, the heavy machine-gun post shown above, anti-tank blocks and even anti-tank ditches. The passage of time has helped to blend these surviving structures into the surrounding undergrowth but, nevertheless, a walk around Cuckmere Haven will still show you how this would area would once have been a formidable 'nut-to-crack' for an invading German Army.

# CLIMPING
## SCHOOL'S SURFACE SHELTER

*Access: By foot along public footpath from Crookthorn Lane.*
*Map reference: TQ 004017.*

*Above: Most people using the footpath past Climping School would assume that this building was part of the normal school buildings. In fact this store room for the schools sports equipment, was once a surface air raid shelter. During an air-raid, about 50 people would have taken cover inside, hence the fact that this design of shelter is often called the '50 Person Shelter'.*

Surface air raid shelters were constructed from a wide variety of designs, the most common of which is the small Anderson shelter. Other examples, such as that above, were constructed from single storey brick and concrete. With the end of the war, such shelters were easily adapted to post war uses, and this has ensured that quite a number have survived to this day. Examples can often be found in the grounds of schools, railway yards, factories, hospitals and even public parks.

Despite the fact that a person was better off in such surface shelters during an air-raid, as the war progressed they had begun to develop a reputation. A bomb or explosion nearby could cause the walls to collapse, bringing the solid, one piece concrete roof crashing down on the shelters occupants!.

Other examples of these '50 Person Shelters' can be found elsewhere in this book, and a surviving Anderson Shelter can be seen in the grounds of Newhaven Fort, Newhaven.

# BODIAM
## 'OLD MEETS NEW!'

> Access: By foot along public footpath in the grounds of Bodiam Castle.
> Map reference: TQ 785255.

*Above: Somewhat dwarfed by the castle at Bodiam is this example of an anti-tank pillbox. These types of pillbox were built for a specific purpose, hence the fact that this example was constructed only yards from one of the largest defensive structures in Sussex!. (Photograph reproduced by the kind permission of Dee Leighton).*

The vast majority of pillboxes built throughout Sussex were based upon designs and plans drawn up by the Directorate of Fortifications, though often local tactical requirements and limitations in the supply of raw materials necessitated modifications to such plans. The plans were executed under the control of the Commander Royal Engineers (CRE) who was attached to the Infantry Division for any specific area and whose task it was to oversee the construction of the defences in his area.

The pillbox shown above is an example of a structure based on the Directorate of Fortifications FW 3/28 plans. Basically the pillbox is divided into two chambers; one for the 2-pounder anti-tank gun, and the smaller for a light machine gun. In this example, the chamber for the 2-pounder gun is on the left-hand side - identifiable by the larger embrasure.

# POLING
## BOMB CRATER

> Location: In private field adjacent to the east side of Poling Street.
> Map reference: TQ 046054.

*Above: Rainwater now gathers in this bomb crater which can be found in a field alongside the main road through Poling. The bomb which caused this crater was almost certainly intended for the Radar Station which had been established at Poling in 1939. In fact, one of the remaining air ministry houses built at the site can just be seen on the left hand side of the horizon.*

On at least four occasions, the village of Poling became the target for German bombers in the early years of the war. The specific target would have been the buildings and masts of the radar station. The records of Sussex Police show 4 air raids for Poling, and give some detail of what occurred on each occasion:

18.08.40. The air raid began at 14.17, and resulted in 2 people being injured. (In fact this was the day that the Luftwaffe caused so much damage at Ford, and other airfields and radar stations across the South of England).

17.01.41. The raid began at 00.30; 2 high explosive bombs and an unknown number of incendiaries were dropped. There were no casualties.

27.05.42. Beginning at 18.00, some 3 high explosive bombs were dropped, leaving 3 people injured.

08.03.43. This raid, timed as 01.20, saw two high explosive bombs dropped, though one failed to explode. No one was injured or killed.

# BARCOMBE CROSS
## ANTI-TANK CYLINDERS

Access: By foot at the junction of School Path and the High Street.
Map reference: TQ 420159.

*Above: These nine anti-tank 'cylinders' would once have been a substantial road block across the road here in the centre of Barcombe Cross. The fact that they have been clumped together on the roadside indicates that they were moved after the war.*

A wide variety of design of anti-tank block existed during the war and the use of a specific type depended on many factors - location, choice of the engineer-in-charge and even the availability of the raw materials.

This type of anti-tank block is termed as the 'cylinder' type by virtue of its shape. Construction was simple with the concrete poured into metal 50 gallon drums on site. Being smaller and lighter in shape, it was not usually intended as a defensive feature, but more the likes of road blocks. Here such blocks would be placed across a road or bridge, allowing troops or Home Guard to control traffic and pedestrians in order to inspect their vehicles and/or documents - they were never expected to stop the heavier German armour in times of attack!. Other examples can be seen at:

Horsham. 7 cylinders line the road side in Denne Road at TQ 172300.

Slaugham. By the entrance to Home Farm, TQ 267281, are 5 such blocks.

# WARTLING
## PYROTECHNIC STORE

> Location: on private farmland to the west of Boreham Lane.
> Map reference: TQ 649068.

*Above: A solitary brick building standing alone in a field near Boreham Lane giving little in clues as to its origin. The only feature which might suggest more than an agricultural use is the heavy steel door built into a steel frame.*

With the arrival of the radar station at Pevensey early in the war came the various defences needed to protect such a site. This building, part of those defences, is a Pyrotechnic Store. It is in fact based upon design plans drawn up by the air ministry for use on dispersal sites at airfields and is one of at least three that survive in this area. The fact that the nearby Pevensey radar station was operated under the control of the RAF explains why a building, designed for use on British Airfields, comes to be found standing alone in a Sussex field!.

Such stores were built of brick, which was sometimes rendered, with a flat felt-covered concrete roof. Inside there would have been upto five shelves. The building itself would have been used to store the ammunition and equipment used by the troops manning the surrounding road blocks, pillboxes and trenches.

# BARCOMBE MILLS

## 'PILLBOX ALLEY'

> Access: By foot along paths and roads in the Barcombe Mills area.
> Map reference: Various.

*Right: One of the many pillboxes at Barcombe Mills. This is an anti-infantry pillbox, and can be found at Pikes Bridge, grid reference TQ 436147. It is an example based on the Type 22 plans drawn up by the Directorate of Fortifications. Of a hexagonal shape, it was intended for 6 men armed with five light machine guns and 1 with a rifle. On the inner wall, opposite the rear entrance is the number A250 (see page 155).*

There is only one term which can be applied to Barcombe Mills - 'Pillbox Alley'. In the immediate area of Barcombe Mills there is no less than 10 surviving pillboxes. Located on the river Ouse, Barcombe Mills had a strategic importance in wartime, covering the approaches up the Ouse alley from the coast at Newhaven and Seaford. For this reason, the numerous bridges over the river and pools at Barcombe Mills became heavily defended with a mixture of both anti-tank and anti-infantry pillboxes. Each pillbox is sited to cover a river crossing, with each bridge often covered by more than one pillbox, and with the aim of making an advance up the Ouse Valley as difficult as possible. There are other such concentrations of pillboxes in Sussex, such as at <u>North Bersted</u> and <u>Arundel</u>, though none have the sheer volume of numbers as at Barcombe Mills.

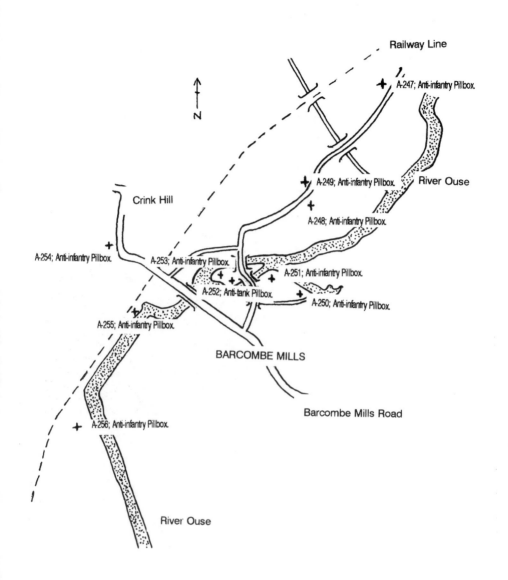

Above: This sketch plan of Barcombe Mills shows the location and type of each of the 10 pillboxes in this area. Some of the pillboxes can be readily accessed, such as A-254 which lies on a public footpath of Crink Hill, whereas others, for example A-252, lie within fenced off fields and have been bricked up. This concentration of defensive structures in fact continues along the west or north banks of the River Ouse in both directions, though the distribution does become more sparse the further one is from Barcombe Mills.

# PEVENSEY
## PEVENSEY RADAR STATION

> Location: On private land between Church Acre Drove & Boreham Lane.
> Map reference: TQ 641071.

The first evidence you will find that tells you that you are approaching the remains of the wartime radar station at Pevensey is a small handpainted sign nailed to the side of a barn. It carries the words 'Pylon Cottages - Private'. In fact, Pylon Cottages are the two remaining Air Ministry houses on this site, and following the concrete road past them, will lead you first to the transmitter block, (now converted to a private bungalow), and then onto the receiver block.

The receiver block itself is heavily protected - large concrete and brick blast walls and earth embankments. This tells us that Pevensey is an example of a East Coast Radar Site, (as opposed to a West Coast). East Coast sites relied on protection for defence, whereas West Coast sites based their defence on dispersal of the buildings. The picture above is a general view of the receiver block, the large blast walls protecting the entrances clearly visible.

All radar stations are based around three main components - the receiver, the transmitter and the power supply. At Pevensey the first two can be easily identified, but the building that would have housed the stand-by generators can no longer be seen, (normally power would have been provided by the National Grid, with generators as back-up). One other important building still remains, but is located in a field some distance east from the main site - the buried reserve. It appears that at Pevensey the buried transmitter and receiver reserves were located together.

*Above: From a distance these concrete lumps give the impression of a lunar landscape. Close up they reveal their true identity : the bases for the 350ft steel transmitter towers. At Pevensey there are remains of all the sixteen original bases for the four towers. Some can even be seen in what is now the garden of the converted transmitter block.*

*Left: A photograph taken in 1947, through the rear window of a moving car, shows only 2 of the 4 steel transmitter towers still standing. It was at this time that the site was passing from the ownership of the RAF to a private landlord.*

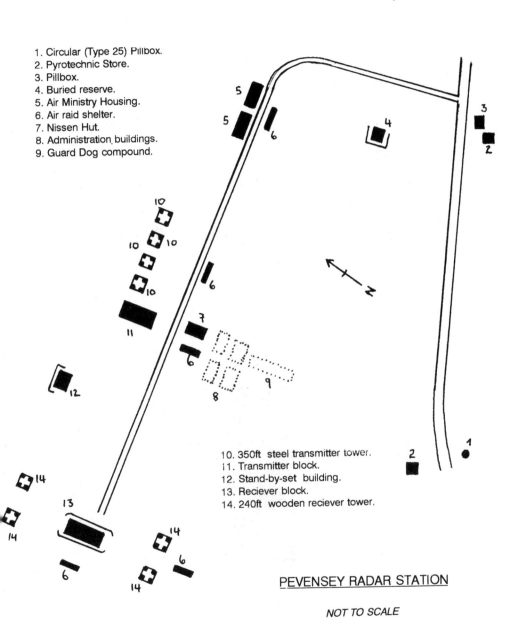

1. Circular (Type 25) Pillbox.
2. Pyrotechnic Store.
3. Pillbox.
4. Buried reserve.
5. Air Ministry Housing.
6. Air raid shelter.
7. Nissen Hut.
8. Administration buildings.
9. Guard Dog compound.

10. 350ft steel transmitter tower.
11. Transmitter block.
12. Stand-by-set building.
13. Reciever block.
14. 240ft wooden reciever tower.

## PEVENSEY RADAR STATION

*NOT TO SCALE*

*Above: Two of the large concrete bases for the wooden receiver towers. These towers, numbering four in total, appear to have been located on each corner of the receiver block, and as with the transmitter towers, all the bases still remain today.*

*Right: A view of what could have been the main plotting room inside the receiver block. It is in here that the operators, often females, would have sat watching the cathode tubes. A signal would have been sent out from the transmitter towers, this pulse of energy either vanishing for ever or hitting an object and bouncing back to be picked up by the receiver towers. By measuring the time between the blips the operator could tell how far away the aircraft was.*

*Above and below: These two poor quality photographs show what happened to the 350ft high steel transmitter towers at Pevensey in 1947. The RAF were pulling out, and the site had been sold to a local man as agricultural land. Demolition teams laced the bases of the towers with explosives, the resulting explosions bringing the towers to earth. Once down, the towers were cut and the metal sold as scrap.*

*Above: By their very nature the radar stations soon became a very hazardous place to be - becoming more frequent destinations for the Luftwaffe. Some protection was provided, and a number of the air raid shelters still survive. This example, (with new occupants), is one of those arranged around the outside of the receiver block. Others can be seen near the location of the administration and transmitter buildings, with two also opposite the ex-Air Ministry houses.*

*Right: Over fifty years of disuse has allowed vegetation to make use of the space between the blast walls and the outside of the receiver block. This space stretches the whole way round the outside of the receiver block.*

# WORTHING
## UNDERGROUND AIR RAID SHELTER

*Location: On Broadwater Green at the east end of Ardsheal Road.*
*Map reference: TQ 144046.*

In the summer of 1937 the British government, awaking to the threat from Nazi Germany, passed the 'Air Raid Precautions (ARP) Act'. This act placed a statutory obligation on local governments to provide their populations with satisfactory protection from air-raids and gas attacks. Generally speaking much of the response by local government was aimed at gas mask and domestic shelters like the 'Anderson Shelter'. Large underground shelters were less favoured on the basis that they risked high casualties from a single incident, and perhaps more importantly, were costly to construct.

The view above shows one of the passages of the Worthing Shelter. Having entered via the main entrance, people would disperse through the shelter, filling it up from the corners furthest from the entrance. Once in their place, everyone would sit on the benches provided (now removed), with their back to the inner wall - in this case on the right-hand side.

*Above: One wonders how many of the people in the vehicles passing this seemingly normal 'bump' on the Green at Broadwater are aware of its true nature?. Located on the south end of the Green the original entrance steps would have faced the shopping parade, but since the war have been filled in - their location can now be seen by a shallow dip in the ground.*

*Left: To gain access into the air-raid shelter today, you have to lower yourself through this manhole cover. This is in fact one of eight emergency hatches that would have been built into the shelter.*

# UNDERGROUND SHELTER

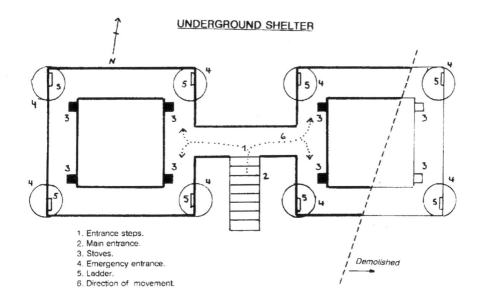

1. Entrance steps.
2. Main entrance.
3. Stoves.
4. Emergency entrance.
5. Ladder.
6. Direction of movement.

Demolished

*Above: A sketch plan of the shelter, which clearly shows how people would have dispersed through it, taking up their positions. On the right-hand side is an area which is shown as demolished - when the main road was widened this end part of the shelter was removed and the tunnels bricked up.*     *Below: A view of the north-west corner of the shelter. On the left it is possible to see the escape ladder, whilst on the right, before the tunnel turns, is what appears to be a drain pipe. This is, in fact, the chimney for one of the 8 paraffin stoves that provided somewhat inadequate heat for the shelter in winter.*

*Below: A view of one of the escape hatches. These were built into the structure to add the rescue of people from the shelter should it suffer a direct or near hit and the main entrance steps become blocked. Even with a lamp, walking through the permanently damp and cold shelter is an eerry experience, and one can easily imagine the unpleasantness of being in such a place, with 200 other people whilst the Luftwaffe bombed the surrounding area!.*

Despite the cost of building such shelters, a number of these underground shelters still exist in the Worthing area. Amongst these, examples can also be found at:

- The carpark at the end of Winton Place in <u>Worthing</u>. A walk round the carpark will lead to the discovery of the emergency entrance hatches.

- Some 400 yards west from <u>West Worthing</u> railway station, on the south side of the track is a small area of scrub. Before the Elm Grove footbridge is another shelter. Here the main entrance was only covered by a sheet of metal, resulting in the shelter being flooded.

- On the main Green in <u>Lancing</u> are two such shelters - their presence also displayed by the characteristic 'bump' in the ground.

# TANGMERE
## BADER ARMS PUBLIC HOUSE

> Access: By foot in Malcolm Road at the junction with Tangmere Road.
> Map reference: SU 904066.

*Right: This side of the sign shows a youthful Douglas Bader wearing a sporting jacket, whereas the other carries a painting of an older Bader dressed in a Tweed Suit. The Bader Arms itself lies in Tangmere Road, and is close to the site of the old airfield living quarters.*

*Further south down Tangmere Road you will come across a small area of grass on a road junction. Here can be found a granite memorial to all those that have served at Tangmere.*

It was early in 1941 that Douglas Robert Stewart Bader began his famous association with the airfield at Tangmere when he was promoted to Wing Commander and made leader of the famous Tangmere Wing of 3 Spitfire Squadrons. He had been at Tangmere previously as the Commanding Officer of No. 242 Squadron flying Hurricanes.

Douglas Bader went from St. Edwards School, Oxford, to the R.A.F. College at Cranwell in 1928. In 1931 he lost both legs when he crashed whilst doing aerobatics, and was invalided out of the R.A.F. in 1933. The onset of war saw him return to active duties with the R.A.F. in 1939, and on February 7th 1940, he joined No. 19 Squadron. He climbed through various commands and Squadrons, till on the 9th August 1941 he shot down two Me 109s, collided with a third, baled out and was taken prisoner. His total tally was 23.

33

# SHOREHAM-BY-SEA
## COASTAL PILLBOX

*Access: By foot along promenade from the West Beach Car Park.*
*Map reference: TQ 202042.*

Almost nothing remains of the wartime coastal defences in Sussex - a symptom of the rapid urbanisation of the South Coast. In particular it is West Sussex which has suffered worst. In fact between Selsey Bill and Shoreham-By-Sea there are believed to be only three remaining pillboxes:

Ferring. A bricked up Type-26 pillbox can be found on Pattersons Walk, TQ 098015.
Lancing. On the beach at South Lancing near the Brighton Road, A259, TQ 178035.
Shoreham-By-Sea. This example can be found on the West Beach Promenade, TQ 202042. The photograph above shows the unique design of the Shoreham Pillbox, which was almost certainly intended for one or two men with a light machine gun.

# SULLINGTON
## BARNS FARM ARMY CAMP

> *Access: By foot along footpath from A283 down Barns Farm Lane.*
> *Map reference: TQ 105135.*

*Above: One of the wooden NCOs and Other Ranks living quarters that still remain at Barns Farm - another example can be seen behind. In the foreground is the original perimeter fence that would once have been patrolled by the ever alert duty guard!.*

The vastly expanding British Army of 1939 led a demand for military accommodation with new army bases springing up across the country. Barns Farm Camp was once a substantial base, housing at different times soldiers of the Canadian and British Armies. Much of the original fabric still remains and still evident are the REME workshops/shed; the parade ground; the ablutions hut and even the cookhouse. The Officers mess, amongst other buildings, has long gone, and its site has become the base of a modern farmhouse. Adjacent to this hut are the tennis courts once used by the Canadian Officers.

At the time of D-Day, Barns Farm Camp had become a Royal Corps of Signals training establishment and anti-aircraft centre. After the war the camp buildings were used as accommodation for initially refugees from wartime Europe, followed by in 1950 displaced Hungarians from the 1950 Hungarian uprising. It then again passed back into the occupation of British Troops on National Service before decommission in the late 1950s.

*Above: The most important building on any camp (apart from the NAAFI) - the cookhouse!. Here the cooks would have prepared and served the food for all those NCOs and Other Ranks on the base - the Officers would have eaten in the Officers Mess.     Below: Tucked away in the southeastern corner of the camp is the office that is all that remains of the petrol store. Near here is the old REME workshop and vehicle store.*

1. Electrical stores and workshop.
2. Lecture room.
3. Control room.
4. Office and stores.
5. Gunnery Staff offices.
6. Lecture room.
7. Lecture room.
8. Cinema and demonstration room.
9. Sports store.
10. Pump house.
11. Settling tank.
12. Irrigation area.
13. Store room.
14. Instruction hut.
15. Pavilion.
16. Quater Masters Office and stores.
17. Playing field.
18. W.O. and Sgts living quaters.
19. Sgts Mess.
20. Fire engine house.
21. Regimental Institute.
22. Regimental Offices.
23. Air raid shelter.

**BARNS FARM CAMP**

BARNS FARM LANE

24. Officers quaters.
25. Officers mess.
26. Parade ground.
27. NCOs and Other Ranks living quaters.
28. Officers stores.
29. Carpenter and barbers shop.
30. R.E.M.E. workshops and garages.
31. Fuel store.
32. Dining room and cook house.
33. Guard Room.
34. Cold store.

*Previous page: A sketch plan showing the original wartime layout of Barns Farm Camp, a layout which even during a brief visit today is still very apparent. Above: The slowly rusting remains of the large REME workshops and vehicle store. Peeling flakes of the original paintwork can still be seen. Below: The parade ground. Where this tarmac expanse would once have resounded to the bawling of the drill sergeant and crashing of soldiers boots, bags of compost now reside.*

*Above: All that remains of the Officers mess - the steps of the main entrance. The brickwork these steps once led upto is long gone - shrubs and weeds taking its place. The Officers quarters have suffered the same fate, though the air-raid shelter behind them has proved a more stubborn structure!.*

*Right: This shell of a Nissen hut is the old Cinema and demonstration room, (location number 8 on the sketch plan). The inside had been stripped out and has since been used to house pigs!. This is one of only two Nissen huts that remain in the grounds of the camp.*

# STORRINGTON
## JEEP REMAINS

Access: *By foot along footpath from South Downs Way, Kithurst Hill.*
*Map reference: TQ 073122.*

*Left: Off the South Downs Way is a small copse hiding these remains of a wartime Jeep.. Here can be seen parts of the chassis and various engine parts including pistons. Also within the undergrowth lie body panels, parts of the springs and even parts of the axles.*

A wide variety of relics and wreckage from the last world war can still be found, even today, scattered across the fields of the South Downs. However, there is little that is as unusual as finding the remains of a wartime jeep!.

Found by chance, these remains are the legacy of the fact that the South Downs were used extensively for training by both the British and Canadian Armies. It is thought likely that this jeep suffered a fatal accident during an exercise and was considered unworthy of the effort of recovery. It would then have been left to rust away, attracting further attention as a target in later exercises.

# WASHINGTON
## EXPERIMENTAL BUNKERS

*Access: By foot along the South Downs Way, west from the A24.*
*Map reference: TQ 107117.*

By late 1940, early 1941, troops of the Canadian Armed Forces had began arriving in Britain, and a large number of their infantry, armoured and engineer units made Sussex their home. As their numbers grew, so did the scope of their services, so much so that by 1942 Windlesham House, at Washington, became the home of the Royal Canadian School of Infantry - a role it played alongside that of being the headquarters of the Department of Petroleum Warfare.

During their time at Windlesham, the Canadian Engineers built a small number of pillboxes on the South Downs nearby. Two, on Highden Hill, had an interesting method of construction. They appear to have been built from large concrete 'breeze blocks' cemented together. On the outside of these blocks are steel plates, about 2 foot square, bolted on in such a way as to leave a 2 inch gap. In turn this gap has been filled with bitumen. It is known that Canadian Engineers had experimented in methods of construction, and it may well be that this had been used as an experimental form of splinter protection - a similar technique has been used in Gibraltar, and bitumen cladding was even once discussed for battleships!.

Another example of a Canadian built pillbox can be seen on Lee Farm at <u>Clapham</u>, north of Worthing. This pillbox, TQ 075115, shows evidence of being shelled.

41

Previous page: Photographed from the South Downs Way is the first of the two Canadian built pillboxes, (TQ 113119). Its new occupants seemed a little uninterested in its unique shape.

Above: The second pillbox can be found south of the South Downs Way at TQ 107117. It too displays a unique shape, but has suffered more from the passage of time with much of its cladding having fallen away and part of its roof collapsed.

Right: The various layers used in the construction - concrete breeze block; steel plates; bitumen and more steel plates.

# GOODWOOD
## AIRFIELD DEFENCE PILLBOX

> Access: By foot along path from the end of Stocks Lane.
> Map reference: SU 872070.

*Above: One of two pillboxes of this design which can be found on the perimeter of the wartime airfield at Goodwood. This one, (SU 872070) lies on the south-western edge of the airfield, whilst on the northern side alongside the Lavant Straight, (SU 876077) is the second.*

This circular type of pillbox is relatively rare, and is in fact based loosely upon the Type 25 plans that were drawn up during the war by the Directorate of Fortifications. These examples at Goodwood have two tiers of loopholes or embrasures, with access through a semi-sunken tunnel. In between the two levels of loopholes is a concrete floor which, on the underside, has what appears to be corrugated iron sheeting (or possibly asbestos). It is likely that this once formed the shuttering for the construction of the floor. Both of the pillboxes have an opening in the roof, though on the example shown in this photograph it is plugged. This opening may have been for one or both of two reasons; to provide for light anti-aircraft guns, or to allow access to the top floor, (there does not appear any way into the top floor from that below). The pillbox here also has what can only be described as a 'sewer-pipe' alongside it, which was probably intended for a light anti-aircraft gun.

# CHICHESTER
## 'DRAGONS TEETH'

> *Access: By foot along a sunken lane adjacent to Brandy Hole Lane.*
> *Map reference: SU 854066.*

*Left: Lining the edge of the public footpath through Brandy Hole Lane are these examples of 'Dragons Teeth'. Whilst the 'Dragons Teeth' can be found at the top of the sunken lane, in the bottom are examples of other types of anti-tank blocks - cubes and cones. In this picture can clearly be seen the size of the concrete foundations that these blocks had, and which was necessary for these structures to form an obstacle of any strength.*

The proper term for anti-tank blocks of this design is 'pimples', but by the end of the war they had adopted the more popular term 'Dragons Teeth'. The latter almost certainly originated from photographs taken at the time of the massive German fortifications on the Atlantic Coast of France and along the Rhine. Here the Germans built anti-tank blocks of this design by the million, and which through the press had become known as 'Dragons Teeth'. Other examples of Dragons Teeth can be seen through out Sussex, such as at:

Amberley. Two examples remain in Church Street at TQ 028132.

Billingshurst. Four remain in the front garden of 99 The High Street, TQ 086257.

Horsham. The remains of at least 15 pimples can be seen across the Causeway, TQ 172304.

# SEAFORD
## UNDERGROUND CONTROL CENTRE

> Access: By foot along access tunnel from south side Eastbourne Road.
> Map reference: TV 513994.

*Right: A gap in the vegetation and some brickwork is all that can be seen that reveals the entrance to the underground control centre at Seaford. This photograph was taken, facing south, from the opposite side of Eastbourne Road near to the Golden Galleon Public House.*

The exact purpose of this underground structure at Seaford is not known, but there are two schools of thought as to why it was built.

The first relates to the nearby concentration of invasion defences at Cuckmere Haven and the important river crossing at Exeat. A number of people believe that this was an underground control room from where the orders and commands were dispatched by radio or telephone to the various pillboxes and defensive positions in the Cuckmere Valley.

The less likely reason for its existence is that it was part of the decoy lighting system set up on the Cuckmere flats. Here a replica of the Newhaven harbour lights was installed, and when an air raid began the lights at Cuckmere were turned on, whilst the actual harbour lights were turned off. In this way it was believed that the bombers would be drawn from their intended target.

*Left: Leading off from the road is the main entrance tunnel. The only other way in or out is through an emergency exit located at the east end of the building and which leads out onto the hillside behind the Golden Galleon. This steel doors can still be found in the entrance beyond the guardroom.*

*Below: This picture shows the main chamber of the control room, which appears to have been built out of a large Nissen hut!. Leading of each end are the smaller offices and rest rooms. As with a large number of surviving wartime structures, the attentions of the graffiti artists has been bestowed on the walls of this room!.*

*Left: The entrance to the guardroom built into the walls of the main entrance tunnel. It is in here that the sentry would have sheltered from a cold night. He would have had telephone contact with the occupants inside the control room, ensuring that those arriving had the necessary authority to enter. The main steel doors are after this control room.*

*Below: On the walls of this small office off the main chamber can be found some of the remains of the original cladding - wooden sheets covered over with fabric sheeting.*

# DALLINGTON
## PETER CROFTS MEMORIAL

Access: By foot along North Road, south from Padgham Corner.
Map reference: TQ 661177.

*Left; A simple wooden cross serves as a memorial to Flying Officer Peter Crofts. The inscription reads: "In grateful remembrance of Peter Guerin Crofts, Flying Officer Royal Air Force, who near this spot gave his life in the Battle of Britain on Sept 28th 1940, and is one of the few to whom so many owe so much".*

On the 28th September 1940 Flying Officer Crofts had been flying a Hurricane of 605 Squadron RAF, when, during a skirmish with enemy fighters over the fields of Dallington, his aircraft was badly hit. Peter Crofts managed to bale out but somehow fell free of his parachute harness and fell to the ground. He was found by local villagers in the grounds of South View Farm to still be alive, but unfortunately died soon after their arrival.

A cross was placed by his mother at the spot where he fell near Padgham Corner, Dallington. Some years later it was discovered in the undergrowth, and the Heathfield branch of the Royal Air Forces Association have tended the site ever since. In the late eighties they had a new cross carved, and which was dedicated at a ceremony attended by Peter Crofts sister.

# TRULEIGH HILL
## TRULEIGH HILL RADAR STATION

Access: By foot along South Downs Way from Tottington Barn.
Map reference: TQ 225106.

*Above: A modern British Telecom tower stands behind the old guardhouse to the radar station at Truleigh Hill. This guardhouse can be found at the end of the approach road to the radar station which leads off from the South Downs Way..*

Truleigh Hill stands on the South Downs overlooking Shoreham-By-Sea, and hosts a large underground RAF facility which is now let out to private contractors for storage. Apart from the underground areas, little does remain of this wartime radar station. The most obvious feature is the old guardhouse, but you can also see some of the original mast bases, tower supports and a few ancillary buildings. This site has been much altered since the end of the war, in that it has now become a communications centre for modern day telephone and mobile phone companies. For this reason, it is perhaps the most difficult of the wartime radar sites to gain access to.

*Above: One of the surviving sets of radar masts. These would have in fact supported the 240ft tall wooden receiver towers. In an adjoining field can be found some small cast iron cable ties which would have held the tension cables used on these towers. Below: One of the few remaining above ground buildings - a ventilation tower. Much of the underground areas remain, and in fact are still in use to this day as secure storage.*

# ISFIELD
## PILLBOX WITH CHIMNEY

Access: By foot along lane to Isfield Church from Isfield Mill.
Map reference: TQ 448183.

*Above: A pretty unique attempt at camouflage has this pillbox fitted with a chimney - but no fireplace!*

This pillbox is based on the Type 24 plans, meaning it is basically an irregular hexagonal strongpoint with the entrance on the longer side. Intended for an anti-infantry role, it would have been operated by 8 men and protected the bridges over the River Ouse at Isfield.

Another typical example of the work of the camouflage officers was the pillbox built in Preston Circus, <u>Brighton</u>, by the end of 1940, and which had adopted the role of a 'newsagents'. The disguise was apparently sufficiently real to confuse a Brighton Councillor who, outraged, tabled a question enquiring who had authorised the newsagent to set up business in such a prominent location - a matter reported without comment in the Brighton & Hove Herald!.

# WASHINGTON
## TRAINING PILLBOX

> Location: In a private copse to the south of the South Downs Way.
> Map reference: TQ 109114.

*Above: This view of the interior of the pillbox built in the woods at Highden Hill, Washington, clearly shows the method of construction used. This strongpoint was not built for any defensive purpose, but as a training aid for those Allied Troops who used this area of the South Downs for their training.*

This is another example of the efforts of the Engineers of the Canadian Army, and was built within what was the grounds of the Royal Canadian Army School of Infantry. The method of construction is extremely basic. The walls are solely built from concrete poured into shuttering in stages. The reason for the stages was to allow the concrete to set without the weight of the mixture above causing the walls to balloon out during setting. It is obvious from this picture that the shuttering used was corrugated iron sheeting. Once the walls had been completed the roof was completed by concrete being poured straight onto more sheets of corrugated iron - in fact these rusting sheets can still be seen in place.

# PEVENSEY
## CIRCULAR PILLBOX

> Location: On private farmland to the east of Boreham Lane.
> Map reference: TQ 653068.

*Above: An excellent example of the pillbox based upon the Type 25 plans drawn up by the Directorate of Fortifications at the early stages of the war.*

As can be seen here, the Type 25 is a circular design intended for the anti-infantry role. Its size ensured that only the bare minimum of men would be able to occupy the pillbox - upto 3 or 4 armed with a mixture of rifles and light machine guns.

This example overlooks a draining ditch east of Boreham Lane near Pevensey, and was almost certainly built as part of the defences for the nearby Pevensey Radar Station. It is likely that a number of other examples exist in the immediate area, as well as at locations throughout Sussex. For example:

Newhaven. Near the old coastguard station at TQ 443001 is a bricked up example.

Seaford. On the golf course at Seaford Head, TV 509980, are a number of Type 25 pillboxes.

Cuckmere Haven. Half way up the valley side at TV 519969, is a sole example.

# SLAUGHAM
## TWO-STOREY PILLBOX

> *Location: In a river bed to the west of Pond Tail Farm, Slaugham Lane.*
> *Map reference: TQ 249277.*

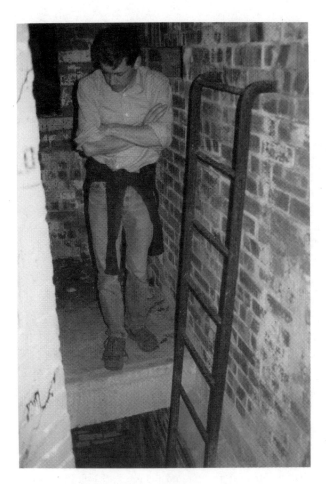

*Michael Boulton stands at the top of ladder from the bottom level which provides access to the top storey. The hole in the floor is relatively narrow, and begs the thought how a soldier with his full compliment of equipment was expected to make a safe entry to the upper floor!. It is this floor that, by virtue of its height above the old river bed, has the clear field of fire over the old river bank and therefore is fitted with the embrasures for the light machine-guns. The lower floor may well have been used for storage or as a rest area by the men based in the pillbox.*

This two-storey pillbox at Slaugham appears to be the only example of its type in Sussex, and in fact is considered to be rare nation-wide. It is basically two Type 26 pillboxes built one on top of the other too create two storeys.

The Type 26 is a square strongpoint built for an anti-infantry role, and would have been occupied by 5 men armed with 4 light machine guns. The reason for having a two storey example maybe found in the fact that this pillbox has been built on the bottom of an old dried up river bed - and by having two storeys the troops on the top level are able to have a clear field of fire over the banks of the dried up river. This would also explain why there is only one embrasure on the lower floor.

# EAST GRINSTEAD
## GRAVES FROM THE WORST AIR RAID IN SUSSEX

> *Access: By foot in the grounds of East Grinstead Cemetery.*
> *Map reference: TQ 397388.*

*Right: The site of the communal grave at Mount Noddy Cemetery in East Grinstead. Here some 22 of the 108 people who died in the raid are buried - it is believed that this is the correct number, though the true amount may never be known. The inscription on the plaque states: "On 9th July 1943, 108 people lost their lives when bombs fell on the town centre. 22 of those people are buried here".*

It was a dull Friday that saw the worst air raid on Sussex take place over East Grinstead on the 9th July 1943. A single Dornier 217 slipped out from the clouds, circled the town, then ran in and dropped eight bombs across London Road and the High Street. The worst carnage was at the Whitehall Cinema where one of the bombs had exploded in the auditorium. Some believe that the pilot had selected a target of opportunity in the shape of a convoy of 20 to 30 army trucks which had drawn up in the car park near Caffyns garage, whilst others say he was aiming at a London bound train. Whatever the target, as the smoke began to clear, the grim body count began - it ended at 108, but it has never been certain that this was the true figure. As well as the dead, some 235 were injured, some seriously.

*Above: Fireman play their hoses on the remains of Bridglands and Rice Brothers in the High Street. In the foreground is Sainsbury's with its shop front damaged (Photograph by kind permission of Mr A. Saunders). Below: The grave of one of those buried in the communal grave at Mount Noddy – Corporal T/2501102 L.W. James of the Royal Army Service Corps.*

# TORTINGTON
## 50 PERSON AIR RAID SHELTER

Access: *By foot along path through grounds of New England College.*
*Map reference: TQ 003053.*

*Right: The entrance to the 50 person shelter at Tortington. In this picture can clearly be seen the toilet that was built into the blast wall. The purpose of the blast wall was to deflect the effects of an explosion nearby away from the shelter entrance.*

As already mentioned, the shape and size of the 50-person air raid shelter has meant that a large number were able to find post-war uses, and as a result a great many have survived even to this day. This example can be found at the American College at Tortington, though during the war the buildings served as a military and civilian hospital. It is probable that other examples of these shelters exist elsewhere in the grounds.

This example is interesting in that, not only has it retained the blast wall that protected the entrance, but that a small toilet has been built into the blast wall - this can be seen on the left hand side of the photograph above. The fact that a toilet has been built into the shelter indicates that at the time of construction the college at Tortington was in civilian use.

# PULBOROUGH
## 25-POUNDER GUN EMPLACEMENT

*Access: By foot along public footpath north from Park Farm.*
*Map reference: TQ 039188.*

*Left: The large embrasure of this 25-pounder emplacement can clearly be seen here, as well as the immense thickness of the walls. The rear of the emplacement is completely open allowing the easy entrance and exit of the 25 pounder gun, or any other similar artillery piece. This emplacement is facing south and covers the railway bridge over the River Arun south of the Stopham Road.*

This type of emplacement appears to be unique to West Sussex, and in particular is found on the defence lines that were built along the banks of the rivers Arun and Adur. There is a little confusion over the exact nature of their use - some state that the emplacements were built to house the British 25-pounder artillery gun, whilst others believe that they were, only initially, built for other artillery pieces - including recovered French guns. See also:
South Stoke. Here a 25-pounder emplacement can be seem at South Stoke Farm, TQ 025102.
Small Dole. At TQ 197133 one can be seen 600 yards south Adur Railway Bridge.
Cornerhouse. Two examples, one each side of Monk Bridge, Bottlings Farm, at TQ 211181.
Offham. 400 yards west of bridge over River Arun at Offham Farm, TQ 027085.

# NEWHAVEN
## COASTAL RADAR SITE

Access: By foot along cliff path below Newhaven Fort, Newhaven.
Map reference: TQ 449000.

*Left: Perched on the cliffs below Newhaven Fort is the building that housed the actual radar equipment. This would have been used to detect and monitor the approach of any enemy shipping should an attack have been made on the Port.*

Nestling on the cliffs below Newhaven Fort is the remains of this coastal radar station, which can be accessed by the cliff top path. It would have been built for the purpose of helping to detect enemy shipping should an attack have been made on the port. In such a situation, the information supplied by the station would have been passed to the port authorities and the battery command post, helping the latter direct the coastal artillery stationed at the Fort and surrounding area.

As well as the actual radar house, along the cliff edge is the monitoring post. Here are the offices and rooms in which the staff of the radar post processed the information received.

*Above: The monitoring post located on the cliffs just west of the radar building. Here were stationed the personnel who processed the information received by the radar equipment. This building is split into a number of offices and rest rooms. On the right is some of the original brickwork of Newhaven Fort.*

*Left: Inside the building that housed the radar itself. In the middle of the floor is the base, whilst in the roof is the aperture through which the radar support passed.*

> Access: By foot along path from Spring Lane towards Franchise Manor.
> Map reference: TQ 664254.

*Above: A simple wooden memorial marks the passing of Flight Lieutenant R.F. Rimmer, who was killed in action during the Battle of Britain on the 27th September 1940. The inscription on the memorial reads "F/Lt R.F. Rimmer, age 21 years, killed in action Sept 27th 1940, deeply mourned by his family".*

Flight Lieutenant Reginald Frank Rimmer flew as a Pilot Officer with number 66 Squadron at Duxford before the war, but was later posted to number 229 Squadron at Wittering. He arrived at this unit just as the Battle of Britain broke out. During late August 1940, 229 Squadron was posted to Bircham Newton, before returning back nearer to the capital early in September. On the 27th September the 21 year old pilot was shot down by enemy fighters over Sussex, his Hurricane fighter exploding in mid-air before he was able to bale out.

He was buried at the Grange Cemetery at Hoylake, Cheshire. After the war his family erected a memorial at Franchise Manor Farm, Burwash, close the actual crash site. Following its deterioration, a new memorial was dedicated at the same site on the 18th June 1977, by the Heathfield Branch of the Royal Air Force Association.

# SELSEY
## ANTI-TANK BLOCKS

> Access: By foot along path west from the West Sands Caravan Park.
> Map reference: SZ 834942.

*Above: A solitary anti-tank block of the 'cube' pattern stands watch over the beach at West Sands Caravan Park on the tip of Selsey Bill. The remainder of the blocks which existed along this part of the coast have either been removed and incorporated into the recent beach defences, or are now part of the edging for the carpark nearby.*

The anti-tank 'cube' is perhaps the larger of the anti-tank blocks, though it often is found to have no foundations - a factor which can no doubt be attributed to its size and weight. Such blocks would once have adorned almost all of the Sussex coastline. For example, by the end of the war, the coast of the Borough of Worthing had some 66 of these anti-tank 'cubes' per mile of its coastline - some 391 in total!. Within the records at Worthing Museum can be found an aerial photograph taken by a Luftwaffe reconnaissance aircraft in 1942, on which it is possible to see a line of such anti-tank blocks stretching corner to corner and completely uninterrupted along the entire Worthing seafront. Other examples are:

Atherington. 50+ at the end of Climping Street, adjacent to beach, TQ 007007.

Selsey. A single example remains by the Broad Rife, south of Ham Road, SZ 832948.

Chichester. Four large 'cubes' lie in the bottom of Brandy Hole Lane, SU 854066.

Bognor Regis. At the end of Sea Road, one example has been built into sea wall, SZ 948994.

# HASTINGS
## PRESERVED SEA-MINE

Access: By foot on the promenade at Rock-a-Nore Road, Old Town.
Map reference: TQ 826095.

*Left: A preserved Second World War naval mine on the promenade off Hastings Old Town. A large number of these mines were used after the war by Trinity House to raise money for various maritime charities.*

*Below: A mine is recovered on the beach at Rustington during the Second World War. It was a common event for a mine to break free from its moorings and be washed ashore to await removal. (Photograph by kind permission of Mrs Mary Taylor).*

# YAPTON
## FAMILY AIR RAID SHELTER

> *Location: In the garden of a private residence in Main Road, Yapton.*
> *Map reference: SU 974033.*

*Above: Gradually being overcome by vegetation is this small family sized air-raid shelter constructed in the grounds of a private house in Yapton.*

From the earliest days of the war, air raid precautions and defences was of immense importance, with the fear of air-raids resulting in the construction of large numbers of air-raid shelters. Due to the cost of municipal shelters, the greater emphasis was placed on smaller, cheaper and easier to construct family sized shelters. These had one more important factor in that they did not concentrate large numbers of people in one place.

The most famous shelter of this size was the Anderson shelter, as well as commercial types such as the steel 'Consul' and pre-cast concrete 'Raidsafe'. This example is a unique design and would have been built at the instigation of the landowner. It has been constructed from brick, and has a blast wall built across the entrance. Inside are wooden racks, presumably which would have acted as beds, and the number of these suggests that the shelter was built for four people.

# NEWHAVEN
## OBSERVATION POSTS

Location: Entrance in grounds of Newhaven Fort, Newhaven.
Map reference: TQ 448000.

*Left: Descending down into the darkness, this tunnel leads from the main area of the Fort at Newhaven to the two observation posts built into the cliff face. The steel lining of the tunnel, installed by the men of 172 Tunnelling Company, Royal Engineers, in 1941, can be seen to be suffering from the effects of the salty sea air - in places it has rusted completely through leading to minor rock falls. (Photographed with the kind permission of Newhaven Fort).*

This tunnel was built in 1941 by 172 Tunnelling Company, Royal Engineers, who from July 1941 to July 1942 were stationed at Tunbridge Wells as part of the 1st Tunnelling Engineers. They were commanded by the Commander Royal Engineers, (CRE), Lt/Col. Hill, RE MC. At that time there were three companies - 170 based in Gibraltar, 171 at Dover and 172 at Tunbridge Wells. This work is likely to have been executed by No. 2 Section, as it is known that they were the part of 172 Company who were working at Newhaven and nearby South Heighton.

Similar works such as this were being carried out across the county. For example troops of the Royal Engineers built a machine gun post just south of the railway line in Shaftesbury Avenue in Worthing. The post was built into a road embankment, and to enable troops to enter the post a tunnel was dug into the post from the east, eventually being about 70ft long.

*Right: One of the two observation posts built into the cliff face below Newhaven Fort. The tunnel itself branches into two, with each branch leading to a separate observation post. From these posts unobstructed views out over the harbour and English Channel are possible. This is the more western of the two posts.*

The tunnels here at Newhaven were dug by hand, with the troops using pneumatic drills or pick-axe. Once dug, the tunnels were reinforced by the use of standard mining ironwork sections - as can be seen in the photograph overpage. These consisted of interleaved galvanised corrugated iron sheets supported by pairs of curved rolled steel joists. In turn these joists were fish plated together at roof level, and braced at floor level.

The same style of tunnelling was employed at the underground naval headquarters at South Heighton. Here the fishplates can be seen to be embossed "GKS-CARDIFF, BRITISH STEEL", indicating that the metal work may have been the product of Guest & Keen Steelworks of Cardiff, supplied in kit form and then bolted together by the Engineers on site.

# FORD
## STANTON SHELTERS

Location: In a private compound adjacent to the B2233 Yapton Road.
Map reference: SU 987027.

*Above: An external view of the Stanton Shelter at Ford. From the other examples present at the same location it is possible to assume that this shelter would have been covered in an earth bank during the war, with only the entrances visible. There are three on this site.*

Like the Anderson shelter, the Stanton Shelter was a commercial brand manufactured to supply the private demand for shelters from those who were not entitled to a free issue of an Anderson shelter. The Stanton Shelter was supplied in pre-cast concrete sections to be erected on site.

Here the Royal Navy has purchased Stanton shelters for use of the airfield at Ford. The shelters in this compound are located in the north west corner of the airfield, in an area which once was the location of part of the airfield ancillary buildings. They have adapted the shelters in the construction of large reinforced brick entrances built at an angle to the entrances.

# RINGMER
## SOLDIERS GRAVES CIRCA 1800

Access: By foot along Broyle Lane at junction with Green Lane.
Map reference: TQ 459144.

*Left: This somewhat different memorial plaque bears the inscription "Site of two soldiers graves, possibly killed in a duel, circa 1800". Even today the graves are still tended to, and can be seen to be marked by the presence of poppies on Remembrance Day, (Photograph by the kind permission of Miss T. Burt).*

Found by accident, this memorial certainly does not fit the criteria of this book, but it was decided to include the picture by virtue of its interesting nature. Located at the junction of two country lanes, the memorial stands in front of two bumps in the ground - the graves themselves!.

The whole area of Lewes and Ringmer is full of interesting historical facts. For example nearby at Lewes was the site of the Battle of Lewes. Fought in 1264 between the forces of Henry III and Simon de Montfort, the site of the battle can be seen from Castle Green in Lewes, and is actually marked by a memorial erected in 1964.

# LYMINSTER
## LOOPHOLES

Access: In the walls of a rest home, A284, Lyminster Road.
Map reference: TQ 028055.

*Right: Hidden behind the vegetation is this loophole built into the wall of a nursing home in Lyminster. From here, a soldier armed with a rifle or light machine gun could create havoc with any enemy attempting to advance north through Lyminster from the coast. At the other end of the same wall, on the northern corner, there is another loophole, placed to cover the approaches from the north.*

Loopholes were possibly the most basic of defensive features used during the Second World War. They could be easily incorporated into any wall, building or feature, and were just as easy to camouflage. In fact how many people who drive past these loopholes at Lyminster each day are aware of their presence?. A solitary soldier, armed with a light machine gun, could feasibly delay a far greater number of attacking troops if he used a well placed loophole. Other examples of loopholes can be seen in Sussex, for example at:

Atherington. On the sea wall alongside Mill Lane are several examples (TQ 011009).

Lyminster. Further loopholes can be found in the wall at corner of Church Road at the junction with the A284, (TQ 025048).

# STONE CROSS
## PEGGY HARLAND MEMORIAL

Access: By foot in the grounds of Stone Cross Church yard.
Map reference: TQ 615044.

*Above: At the roadside by Stone Cross Church is the village war memorial. Not all the names on the memorial relate to soldiers killed in action, for the last, Peggy Harland, was a young girl guide killed as the result of an air-raid on Eastbourne.*

Peggy Harland was a member of the 1st Stone Cross Company of the Sussex Girl Guides. On the fateful day she had been in Eastbourne visiting friends when a high explosive bomb fell on the building she was in, entombing her and six others. The rescue squad worked for 24 hours before they were able to extricate Peggy, and it was found that her feet could not be moved. With the sirens blowing and a 'dog-fight' in progress overhead, one foot and one leg were amputated in an effort to free her. As long as she had been conscious, Peggy remained absolutely cheerful and she made no fuss. Once freed, she was taken to hospital where she regained consciousness and again made no complaints or grumbles during the next 24 hours. At the end of this period, Peggy died from the effects of delayed shock. It was also found in hospital that her back was broken.

For the courage and strength she had shown upto her death, Peggy Harland was awarded the Girl Guides Gilt Cross, this being announced in the national press on the 2nd August 1941.

> Access: By foot along path through the Pett Level Conservation Area.
> Map reference: TQ 891138.

*Left: The concrete mounting base for the spigot mortar. At the time of construction, a deep trench would have been dug all round the concrete base in which the operating troops would have stood. A shallow dip in the ground around the concrete is all that remains of this trench.*

The spigot mortar, also known as the 'Blacker Bombard', was capable of hurling an explosive projectile some 400 yards. The emplacement on which it fitted was made from concrete poured into a 'thimble' of some 4 foot high and 3 foot wide. The top of this 'thimble' was rounded, and fitted with a high quality stainless steel pin. The mortar would be placed onto the metal pin, which in turn enabled the mortar to be spun through a full 360 degrees - giving a completely uninterrupted field of fire. Such concrete bases can be found throughout the country, by bridges, important road junctions and even alongside coastal artillery batteries (as is the case here).

One Sussex town which is known to have had a large number of these weapons was East Grinstead. Here some 12 spigot mortar bases were installed by important road junctions and bridges to protect the approaches to the town from the South and East.

# SEAFORD
## SURFACE AIR RAID SHELTER

Access: By foot along the side of Eastbourne Road in private garden.
Map reference: TV 503993.

*Above: Yet another type and example of a surface air raid shelter, this time on the roadside beside the Eastbourne road in Seaford.*

This shelter has been altered since the end of the war - the nearest entrance has been bricked up, whilst at the opposite end the entrance and some of the brickwork has been removed to allow new access to the house behind. In the event of an air-raid people would have filed in through both entrances, and passed down the shelter till meeting in the middle. Once inside they would have sat down on the benches provided along the back wall.

Other shelters exist in Seaford, for example at:

TV 494995. A characteristic 'bump' in the ground behind the offices in Sutton Road denotes the location of an underground shelter, though its entrance is blocked.

TV 483988. A surface shelter could be found on the waste ground near Steyne Road, though at the time of going to print, this site was being cleared for development, with the result that this shelter will almost certainly have vanished.

> *Access: By foot in the grounds of the Dragon Inn Public House.*
> *Map reference: TQ 229327.*

*Above: Hidden away in the corner of the garden of the Dragon Inn at Colegate is this small, unique air-raid shelter. There is nothing unusual in the presence of such an air-raid shelter, but what is different is the manner in which the shelter was built.*

It was on a dull overcast night in September 1940 that the peace and tranquillity of the small Sussex village of Colegate was ripped apart by the arrival of the German air force. A single bomber made its way across the village, unleashing its stick of bombs which were to kill some five people. The first bomb fell on the house of the District Nurse, which was next to the pub, and others fell on the Post Office and village hall. This first explosion destroyed the District Nurse's house, and seriously injured her.

It appears that following the air raid, the then landlord of the village pub decided to review the lack of shelters in the village. Having decided to provide a shelter for the villagers in his garden, the landlord turned to the best available source of bricks for building such a shelter. This was found in the form of the rubble from the District Nurse's house and the post office. The landlord, however, was incensed when after collecting the bricks free of charge, the builder then charged £25 for their contribution to its construction!.

# HASTINGS
## DUNKIRK LIFEBOAT MEMORIAL

> Access: On display in the Life Boat Station, Hastings Old Town.
> Map reference: TQ 825094.

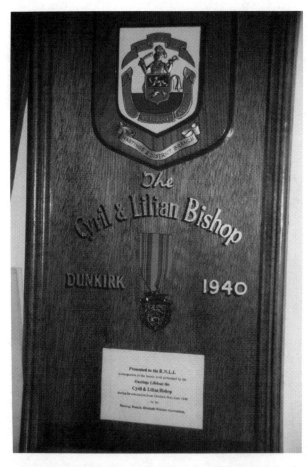

*Left: This memorial to the old Hastings Lifeboat, the 'Cyril & Lilian Bishop', can be found on the wall of the Hastings Lifeboat Station. It was awarded in recognition in the lifeboats service at the time of the Dunkirk evacuations. The inscription on the plaque reads: " Presented to the R.N.L.I. in recognition of the heroic work performed by the Hastings Lifeboat, 'The Cyril & Lilian Bishop' during the evacuation from Dunkirk, May-June 1940, by the Hastings Branch, Dunkirk Veterans Association".*

As would be expected, wartime was a busy period for the Hastings Lifeboat. At 9.29 pm on the 9th September 1939, for example, the *'Cyril & Lilian Bishop'* was put to sea to aid the Dungeness lifeboat *'Charles Cooper Henderson'*. A R.A.F. Anson aircraft had ditched in the sea about seven miles south-west of Dungeness - it was still afloat and its four man crew were gathered on its upper surfaces.

The 'Cyril & Lilian Bishop' found the aircraft at 10.40, having been abandoned by its crew and took it in tow, arriving at Hastings with the aircraft at 1.30 am. For their efforts, the crew of the Hastings Lifeboat were awarded £28 14s. 6d. The only flaw in the rescue operation had been the fact that no one had told the Dungeness lifeboat that both the crew and plane had been recovered - they continued searching till 1am!.

# PETT LEVEL
## EMERGENCY COASTAL BATTERY

Access: By foot through the grounds of Pett Level Nature Reserve.
Map reference: TQ 891135.

*Above: The Battery Observation post at Pett Level stands watch over the nearby beaches. The Battery itself consisted of several integrated parts - the gun house, the observation post, mortar sites and other assorted defensive features. Such batteries were intended to be self sufficient for as long as possible in times of attack.*

It was following the Allied evacuation from the beaches of Dunkirk that the reality of Britain's isolation really instigated the massive building programme of coastal defences. Part of this building work, was the construction of large numbers of Emergency Coastal Artillery Batteries. Each one had an individual layout, with some being relatively small and basic affairs, whereas others could be called forts in their own right. This Emergency Battery at Pett Level is located on a small isolated hill in the middle of the flat levels behind the beach. Often such Emergency Batteries were equipped with either 6", 5.5", 4.7" or 4" artillery pieces that were sourced from large stocks that were held by the Royal Navy. The battery at Pett Level appears unusual in that it was built for one artillery piece, whereas it was the norm for such batteries to consist of two guns.

*Above: A rear view of the two-storey battery observation post. It is from here the ranges and directions of a target would have been relayed to the gun crews in the gun house. It is unfortunate, but at some stage the steps to the top floor have been removed, though it is still possible to see that the mounts for the range finding equipment are still present.     Below: The remains of a gun pit, possibly for heavy machine gun, or light anti-aircraft gun. The remains of what is believed to be the search light mount can be seen on the opposite side of the Battery Observation Tower.*

*Above: The gun floor, with the large concrete gun mount in the centre. Inspection of the gun house reveals that a roof once existed over the gun floor as far as the gun mount to provide some degree of protection to the gun crews - both against the elements and any passing enemy aircraft.*

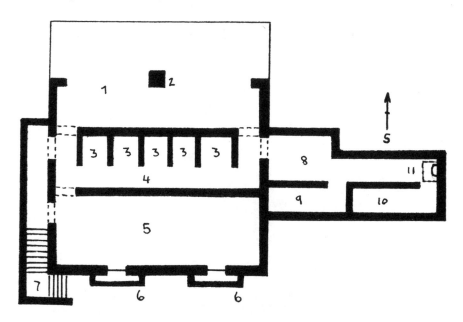

Plan of the Pett Level gun house: 1; Gun Floor, 2; Gun mount, 3; Ammunition recesses, 4; Passage, 5; War shelter, 6; Protected window, 7; Entrance steps, 8; Passage, 9; Shell store, 10; Cartridge store, 11; Emergency entrance.

*Above: At the rear of the gunhouse is the 'war shelter'. Here there is evidence that this large room was partitioned into smaller sections, possibly to provide separate offices for the likes of the commanding officer, communications section or for various rest rooms.*

*Left: Backing onto the rear wall of the gun floor are five ammunition recesses. It is in these that the ammunition for the gun would have been stored ready for action. As the supplies from here were depleted, further shells would have been brought forward from the reserve stores.*

*Left: A view of the passageway past the shell and cartridge stores - this is marked as 8 on the sketch plan. At the end bolted to the wall is a metal ladder leading upto the emergency exit hatch. This emerges onto the hillside between the gun floor and the battery observation post.*

*Right: Inside the shell store. As with the identical adjacent cartridge store, a single shelf decorates the room. It is on and below this that the shells would have been stored, waiting to replenish those used from ammunition recesses behind the gun floor.*

# WIGGONHOLT
## TRAINING TRENCHES

> Access: By foot along public footpath through woodland from the A283.
> Map reference: TQ 061163.

*Above: Falling autumn leaves gather in this shallow dip that is all that remains of what was once a trench used by infantry in their training. Along the left-hand side of the trench can be seen metal poles placed at regular intervals - these may have once supported barbed wire entanglements, or camouflage netting.*

This bit of the Sussex countryside lies in an area that throughout the Second World War was the home to a large number of infantry camps - for example the nearby grounds of Parham House which was home to troops from the Canadian 1st, 2nd and 3rd Army Divisions. In the lead up to operations such as Dieppe or D-Day these troops would have trained relentlessly, making much use of the surrounding countryside. In a small sand pit nearby could be found an abandoned tank, presumably used for training, which was not removed until the late 1950s.

Another example of such trench systems can be seen in the grounds of the Chalk Pits Museum at Amberley, TQ 028122. This area was used by regular troops, as well as by the Commandos of both the British and Canadian Armies who valued the steep chalk cliffs the location offered. In these trenches it is still possible to find the remains of spent .303 rounds.

# BILLINGSHURST
## UNDERGROUND OBSERVER CORPS POST

Access: By foot in compound adjacent to layby on the A272.
Map reference: TQ 095258.

*Left: The reason why these post-war underground observer corps are so hard to recognise - little can be seen above ground. This is the entrance, which is only about a square yard in size, behind which can be seen a few air vents and tubes for the various probes. The post here at Billingshurst first opened in 1925, and was moved to the present location in February 1949. The underground post was built in June 1958, and was decommissioned some 10 years later in October 1968.*

These post-war observer corps posts are worth a mention by virtue of the fact that a great many still survive in Sussex. With the coming of the cold war, and the nuclear age, the Royal Observer Corps was to undergo dramatic changes, the not least of which was to go underground. From the mid-1950s a series of underground observation posts, intended to monitor the explosion and fallout from nuclear explosions, were built nation-wide. A crew of three men were intended to operate each post, with the vast majority being completed at the height of the cold war between 1958 and 1964. A grand total of 875 such posts were completed. Such posts remained in service in varying numbers until the Royal Observer Corps was disbanded in November 1991. Other examples can be seen at:

<u>Crowborough</u>. Established 1925, went underground in October 1960. TQ 506296.

<u>Newick</u>. Established 1925, went underground at TQ 417227 1961 and closed 1968.

<u>Midhurst</u>. Established during 1925. Underground post opened 1962 at SU 864198.

*Above: The inside of the main chamber, which has suffered the passing of time by becoming flooded and covered in graffiti. It is not known whether the beds are part of the original fittings, but they certainly seem to have the appearance of being government issue!. Left: Access to the post is down this steel ladder, bolted to the side of a shaft which is some 15ft deep. At the bottom of the shaft are two doors; to the left is the door to the chemical toilet, whilst straight ahead is the doorway to the main chamber.*

*Above: A reconstruction of what the interior of such a post may once have looked like. This can be seen at the Royal Observer Corps display at Newhaven Fort. (Photograph produced by kind permission of the director of Newhaven Fort). Left: One of the vents through which a monitoring probe would have been placed - possibly the Fixed Survey Meter Probe. These posts were built in clusters within a small area in an effort to provide a satisfactory triangulation of plots.*

# SHOREHAM-BY-SEA
## DEFUSED GERMAN BOMB

> *Access: On display in the main terminal building, Shoreham Airport.*
> *Map reference: TQ 205053.*

*Right: Standing on a wooden plinth in the main terminal building at Shoreham Airport is this German 250Kg bomb. The inscription on the plaque reads: "Presented to Shoreham Airport by the Officer Commanding 49 (EOD) Squadron, Royal Engineers, on completion of the clearance of the airport on 24 February 1982. This WW2 German 250kg bomb was found during a routine clearance task, and was rendered safe by the BDO and crash crew of 49 (EOD) Squadron RE on 11 February 1982.*

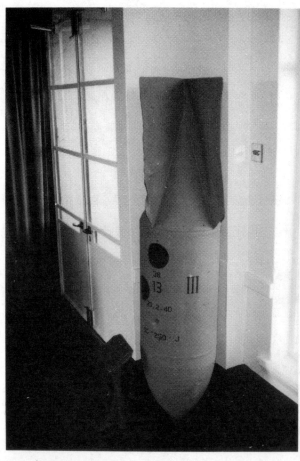

Major A.L. Shaw remembers his time as the Commanding Officer of No. 2 Section, 222 Field Company Royal Engineers, during the hectic days of 1940. The 130 men of his unit were employed on the construction of the anti-invasion defences on the coastal area between Shoreham and Worthing: "My unit did much work with the Canadian Divisional Engineers who were arriving in Sussex. They had brought with them oil pipeline drilling equipment, which enabled us to drive 4" diameter pipes into the ground. These pipes were filled with ammonal explosive, creating a device we called 'pushpipes' or pipe-bombs'. They were placed by the Canadians under roads and runways, with the resultant crater designed to render the road or runway useless to the enemy!." It was at the same time as this bomb was discovered that Engineers uncovered a number of these 'pipebombs' buried under Shoreham Airport, subsequently closing the airfield!.

# HALNAKER
## ANTI-AiRCRAFT BATTERY

Access: By foot up Old Mill Road from Warehead Farm, off the A285.
Map reference: SU 920096.

*Above: Standing on the top of Halnaker Hill, this anti-aircraft emplacement does not seem to be much out of place in the shadow of Halnaker windmill. The hill itself lies in front of the South Downs, and stands out over the coastal plains on which lie the wartime airfields of Westhampnett, Tangmere, Apuldram and Merston.*

The presence of these anti-aircraft emplacements near the Halnaker windmill is well documented, but what isn't recorded are the few interesting features that can be found on inspecting the site. Near the windmill are two gun emplacements built for light anti-aircraft guns. Their presence here is no doubt a consequence of the commanding position the site has overlooking the various wartime airfields below. Further behind the two emplacements is a third structure, with a somewhat less obvious purpose. This structure is built along the same design as the two emplacements, but is completely capped by a solid concrete roof, in the middle of which is a single opening. Beside the structure is a metal tank, from which a single pipe runs through a pump mechanism into the structure ending immediately below the single hole in the roof. It is thought that this building was used to lay down a protecting smoke screen for the anti-aircraft guns as they carried out the valuable task of protecting the airfields.

*Above: The second of the anti-aircraft gun emplacements - interesting in that a completely different brick has been used. Both of the emplacements have the remains of the gun mounts inside, with access gained through doorways with blast walls. Below: Other remains can be found at this site - here a hardstanding which may once have been the base of a Nissen Hut, or the location of another gun.*

Above: A view of the third structure which lies at the north side of Halnaker Hill. On the left-hand side is the large metal tank, connected to the inside of the building by a single metal pipe. Left: A view of the solid concrete roof of this structure. Clearly seen is the single entrance hatch into the building. In the back ground, the dramatic views show the high isolated position that these emplacements occupy - this possibly being the single reason why the laying of a smoke screen from this third building might be needed. On the same note, it might be that the distinctive landmark created by the windmill would need shrouding from enemy aircraft by such a smoke screen.

*Above: A view of the sparse interior of the third structure.*

*Left: This is the end of the pipe that emerges below the gap in the roof. The pipe itself originates from the end of the large metal tank, passes through a pump mechanism and various valves, before ending here. The soot on the walls suggests that a flammable liquid is burnt at the end of the pipe, creating clouds of smoke which in turn billow out through the roof opening and envelope the adjacent gun emplacements and/or windmill.*

Location: On the shoreline at the bottom of Bailey's Brow.
Map reference: TV 544965.

*Above: Resting alongside the wreck of the tramp steamer 'Oushla' is the remains of the Submarine U-211, (Reproduced by the kind permission of the Seaford Museum).*

Even today, a walk along the cliff top at Bailey's Brow in the right conditions might permit you a view of some of the remains of the wreck of this submarine. The last vestiges of this craft can be seen at the base of the cliffs here at Bailey's Brow, which is the sixth of the Seven Sisters, (if counting from west to east towards Eastbourne).

It was at the end of the First World War, that the U-211 was in tow to France as 'spoils of war', when the tow line broke allowing the unmanned submarine to drift towards the cliffs. Unable to regain control of the submarine, it rammed bow first into the remains of another wreck, the tramp steamer *'Oushla'*, hitting it in the boiler-room. The *'Oushla'* had lain at the bottom of Bailey's Brow since 1916 when it is believed to have run aground in bad weather.

# HALLAND
## BLACK OUT MARKINGS

Access: On road bridge on the B2192, at White Lion Farm.
Map reference: TQ 496156.

*Right: The bridge on the B2192 at White Lion Farm. Each of the four bridge posts have evidence of black -out markings on them, though this is the best example.*

It was on the 1st of September 1939, just before the war began, that Britain was placed under a blackout, a period of darkness that was to last for many a year to follow. Householders got to work straight away, only to soon realise that maintaining a complete black-out was not going to be as easy as one thought!. Indeed , many were shocked to find that a single layer of material would not block out all the light from a well-lit room.

Early in November 1939, the period of blackout for each day was made in regulations as being half an hour after sunset to half an hour before sunrise. This blackout was to be enforced by a strict set of emergency regulations set by the government, and governed by both the Police and A.R.P. Services.

# SULLINGTON
## WORLD WAR ONE SUBMARINE MEMORIAL

> Access: By foot in Churchyard of Sullington Church, Sullington Lane.
> Map reference: TQ 098132.

*Left: There are not many churchyards that posses a memorial to the Captain and crew of a First World War Submarine. This memorial can be seen by the main gate to the churchyard of Sullington Church.*

The submarine E-24 was a minelaying submarine of the E-class. She was built by Vickers Ltd at their Barrow-in-Furness yard, and launched on the **9th** January 1916. With her crew of 3 Officers and 27 ratings, the E-24 was to have a short and somewhat blighted career. On her first patrol she fired 1 torpedo at the German auxiliary vessel 'Aneland', but missed. On the 7th March 1916 she laid 20 mines, designated Field 103, 12 miles south of Hegioland. On the 21st March 1916, she sailed from Harwich on another mine laying operation - it was to be her last mission. Her intention had been to lay more mines to the south-east of Field 103, but on the 24th of March she was posted as lost at sea, both the submarine and crew lost without trace.

*Above: A view of a sister ship of the E.24. This is the submarine E.46 shown here underway at harbour stations, Malta, 1918. Note the clear view of the mine tube holes. (With acknowledgement to the Royal Navy Submarine Museum, Gosport).    Below: A close-up view of the description on the side of the war memorial in Sullington churchyard.*

*Above: Lt Cdr Naper seen standing on the deck of another submarine, the C14. The photograph was taken in 1913/1914 whilst this C-class submarine was docked alongside a supply ship at Blyth. Naper is in the centre, (With acknowledgement to the Royal Navy Submarine Museum, Gosport). Naper joined the Royal Navy on the 30th October 1900 as Midshipman, becoming Lieutenant-Commander in June 1914.*

There is still much mystery surrounding the sinking of the E-24 because with the exception of a reported sighting of the submarine near the English coast on the 21st March 1916, she was never seen again.

However, in 1973 the German recovery firm Harms discovered a wreck in some forty metres of water about 10 miles north-west of Hegioland. Believing it to be a wartime German U-boat they commenced salvage operations. Once hauled to the surface, it turned out to be the wreck of the E-24, with the bodies of 4 officers and 31 men still on board. The damage to the bow and the fact that the hatches were open suggested that the submarine had struck a mine whilst on the surface, possibly one it had just laid. The remains of the men were buried at Ohlsdorf Cemetery, the boat broken up and some artefacts placed on show at Cuxhaven.

# WEST CHILTINGTON
## MUNITIONS FACTORY

> Location: In the private grounds of a farm off Southlands Lane.
> Map reference: TQ 093177.

*Above: Tucked away in the corner of a farm yard is this small industrial unit, which at the outset of the Second World War was put to use in the manufacture munitions, though exactly what type of ammunition or weapon was manufactured here is not known. It is also known that other buildings in West Chiltington, nearer the Roundabout, were used in the production of munitions, (Photograph produced by the kind permission of Mr A. Oliver).*

This is an example of the remains of the vast industrial effort that occurred throughout the Second World War. With total war the greater majority of a nations industry is switched to the production and manufacture of military equipment - car producers began manufacturing tanks; garden equipment suppliers now made steel helmets and even food manufacturers began to switch to military supplies. The location and nature of many of these once important industrial buildings has often been forgotten, and current investigation relies heavily on the long memories of local residents - as in the case above!. Another example of the location of a wartime factory is:

Storrington. Off Chantry Lane is the old Marley works, now split into small industrial units. Pre-war this site was employed in manufacturing bricks and tiles, but during the war was switched to military supplies - including parts for the famous D-Day Mulberry Harbours.

> Location: In field between the B2139 and Crossgate Cottages.
> Map reference: TQ 034133.

*Above: A pair of tractors mark the last resting place of a Hurricane fighter that crashed in the corner of this field below the South Downs at Crossgates, Amberley.*

On the 20th February 1941, a Hawker Hurricane crashed near Crossgates, Amberley. The aircraft involved was a Mark 1 example with the serial number R2687. The plane was part of 302 Squadron Royal Air Force, and was piloted by a Polish Airman, Pilot Officer E. Pilch. From eye-witness accounts it appears that the plane had been involved in a high altitude dog fight with German aircraft, when at about 10.30 am, the plane was seen to begin to fall from about 15,000ft. The plane hurtled to the ground, impacting at some speed. The pilot never baled out, and as a result many believe that the crash was the result of oxygen failure.

On hitting the ground the plane buried itself to a depth of some 30ft, and burnt out almost immediately. The remains of the aircraft were recovered by a maintenance team sent from RAF Faygate near Horsham. It was then that the pilots body was recovered. Local rumour has it that the pilots head was never recovered, and that it was found some weeks later in a hedge near the crash site by a local man out walking his dog. Whatever the truth in this, P/O Pilch lies in the National Polish War Cemetery.

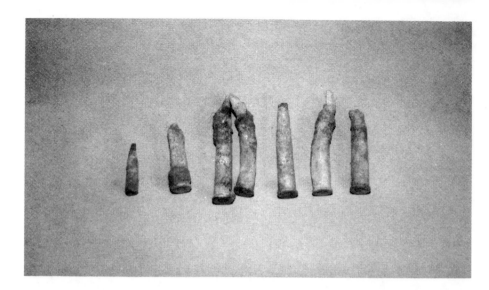

*Above: Some of the unexploded rounds that have been found by local farmers at the crash site. One of the eyewitnesses states that the impact of the crash set of the remaining ammunition the plane was carrying, with the whole area resounding to the crackle of exploding .303 rounds.    Below: Some of the multitude of small pieces that are turned up on the crash site each time it is ploughed. In fact the farmer states it is possible to detect the crash site from the Downs as a discoloured area of soi* immediately after ploughing.*

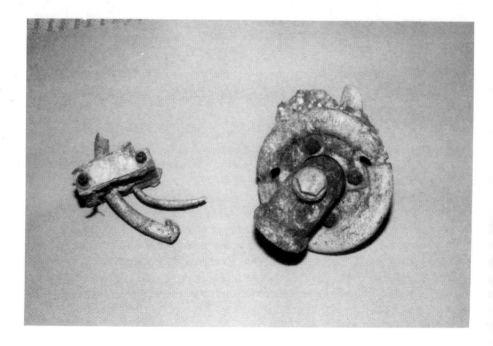

> Access: By foot along the cliff top path east from Newhaven Fort.
> Map reference: TV 443999.

*Left: Balancing precariously on the cliff top, this post has markings on three sides. On the north side, (visible here), is the legend "WD, M 22". On the west facing side it is possible to read "WD No 222", whilst on the south facing side is "To Medium Low Tide".*

This marker can be found on the very edge of the cliffs above Newhaven harbour - in fact the western harbour arm can be seen stretching out into the Channel in the background.

It is almost certainly part of the construction work that took place at Newhaven during the later part of the 19th Century, or early in the 20th. Similar examples of these markers can be found at:

Chichester. Around the grounds of the barracks on Broyle Road are a number of such markers, for example at the junction of Broyle Road and Wellington Road, grid reference SU 861062.

# SOUTHBOURNE
## THE SMALLEST AIR RAID SHELTER IN SUSSEX!

> Location: Under the north side platform of Southbourne Railway Station.
> Map reference: SU 771059.

*Right: Sandwiched under the northside platform is this the smallest air raid shelter in Sussex!. Barely able to accommodate two adults, it had originally been constructed to house the single member of platform staff that would have worked at Southbourne during the war. Despite its size, it is strongly built and is even equipped with a blast wall - which did nothing to aid access in and out of this somewhat confined space. The shelter has now been relegated to the position of storeroom!.*

Despite being possibly the smallest shelter in Sussex, this structure would still have served a useful purpose. This part of the railway was frequently the subject of attack from passing German planes by virtue of its obvious appearance and location sandwiched between the towns of Chichester and Portsmouth.

Almost without exception all the stations within the old Southern Railway were equipped with air-raid shelters. Another example of this can be seen at <u>Worthing</u> Central Railway Station. Here, under platform 3, an air raid shelter was created from the old cellars. Wooden seats were provided and an emergency escape hatch was built into the ceiling, emerging out onto platform 3 - this can still be seen today near the station buffet.

# BOPEEP BOSTAL
## ARTILLERY SHELL REMAINS

Access: By foot along the South Downs Way east from Bopeep carpark.
Map reference: TQ 493051.

*Right: This somewhat unusual weight can be found hanging on a gate on the South Downs Way near Bopeep Car Park on Bopeep Hill. To reach the gate you must walk west from the carpark along the route of the South Downs Way.*

As the volume of British and Canadian Troops billeted in Sussex continued to mount, so did the proportion of the Sussex Downs that was declared out of bounds to the local population. Not even the demand for food supplies in Britain was able to stop much of the South Downs becoming part of the vast military training areas. Here the army would carry out their manoeuvres, build their defences and carry out testing of their artillery pieces and other assorted weapons.

Even today if you go on a walk on the South Downs it is possible to find evidence of the fact that so many troops once trained on these fields. This simple weight stands testimony to the fact that throughout the war years the South Downs resounded to the banging and exploding of artillery pieces on the various ranges.

# LANCING
## LANCING CARRIAGE WORKS MEMORIAL

Location: In memorial garden alongside South Street, Lancing.
Map reference: TQ 183042.

*Above: With the closure of the large Southern Railways depot at Lancing, a new home was required for the works own war memorial. It was felt that the natural choice was to place the memorial at its current location - next to the Lancing War memorial in South Street.*

As with any large organisation the Southern Railway was required to release manpower from its workforce for service with the Armed Forces - something which it did throughout both the world wars. The result of this conscription was that a number of the Lancing Works staff died whilst on active service, all of whom were remembered on the work's own war memorial.

Despite the loss of so much of its workforce to conscription, the Lancing carriage works still did sterling service in the Second World War. For example in the first months of 1939 the depot converted 27 coaches and 3 restaurant cars into hospital trains. Over the coming years, amongst other things, the depot produced 100 petrol tanks; manufactured parts for the 25-pounder guns; 2-pounder breach mechanisms; tail plane units; motor launches for the Admiralty; and even bent some 3,000 old rails into 'hairpin' road blocks!.

Today almost nothing exists to remind us of the presence of the Lancing Carriage Works - except their own war memorial.

# COLEGATE
## GUIDES 'V.C.' MEMORIAL

Access: By foot on the entrance wall of Colegate Church, Forest Road.
Map reference: TQ 232328.

*Above: The Bronze Cross. It would have had a red ribbon and was only given for instances of the greatest heroism, where extreme risk of life has been faced. Right: The Colegate war memorial on which can be found the name of Heather Barnes. It lies on the wall immediately inside the main entrance to the Church in Colegate.*

Heather Barnes was a volunteer V.A.D. Nurse, who at the time of her death was Captain of the 1st Colegate Company of the Sussex Girl Guides. One evening in September 1940 she was, in her capacity as a volunteer nurse, attached to the first aid party in Colegate. One night a severe air-raid developed over the village, during which the Guide Association citation states Heather Barnes showed amazing courage and endurance. For her work, Heather Barnes was posthumously awarded the Girl Guide's Bronze Cross. The 1941 Girl Guides Policy, Organisation and Rules book states that the Bronze Cross is the highest award given to a Girl Guide for gallantry.

# GUIDES' "V.C." FOR DEAD NURSE

## Guides 'V.C.' for girl who died bravely

*Above: Acts of bravery such as that shown by Heather Barnes always received much coverage in the National Press, as these two headlines show. Appearing in the national press in November 1941, both of these articles went on to explain that this was only the second time since the beginning of the war that the Bronze Cross had been awarded.*

During the air raid, on the 9th to 10th September 1940, when a string of high explosive bombs were dropped across Colegate, destroying the Post Office and District Nurses house, Heather Barnes attempted to reassure the elderly and frightened village residents. She could not be persuaded to take cover, and continued going from house to house. When the bomb fell onto the District Nurses house Heather Barnes and two other V.A.D. nurses scrambled through the wreckage rescuing the District Nurse. Together they carried the nurse to the village hall, where whilst attending the District Nurses wounds, a bomb fell. Heather Barnes received injuries from which she died a few hours later.

At the time Heather Barnes was only 20 years old. The Senior warden had the following to say of her: "I was struck by the splendid behaviour in what must have been, for a young girl, a terrible experience. I can honestly say I have known men who could not have done any more, and I consider she upheld the best tradition of the Girl Guides".

The Bronze Cross was given to the parents of Heather Barnes in a private interview by the Queen at Buckingham Palace on the 22nd October 1941.

102

# NORTH BERSTED
## INFANTRY SECTION POST

Location: On private agricultural land to the north-west of Berry Lane.
Map reference: SU 925016.

*Right: The interior of the North Bersted Infantry Section Post. From the state of the structure it is assumed that it was built from local materials to a local specification - the roof is not level; the embrasures are too close to the roof; and the fire supports are not level!. An average sized person would have difficulty in finding a comfortable position at one of the embrasures, let alone 8 fully armed troops whilst under attack!.*

An infantry section post is, as its name suggests, intended to give a degree of protection to the men of a specific section. Inside such a structure they would operate their weapons - rifles or light machine-guns whilst still being able to have a reasonable field of fire. For this reason a section post would normally be built to accommodate a number of troops with embrasures on all sides of the structure. In fact, the section post here is part of a complex of defences. Still in existence in the surrounding fields are two other pillboxes and a single heavy machine-gun post. Another example of an infantry section post can be seen at:
**Arundel.** In the grounds of Home Farm, TQ 016077, which is part of the Castle Estate.

# RICKNEY
## UNIQUE ANTI-TANK BLOCKS

> *Access: By foot along Glynleigh Road at Bridge Farm Road Bridge.*
> *Map reference: TQ 627069.*

*Above: On the north side of the river by Bridge Farm Road Bridge, this line of anti-tank blocks spread out away from the road.*

These anti-tank blocks, whilst of an interesting design, show quite clearly the method of their construction. This has basically occurred in two stages. In the first part the semi-triangular caps were made in a wooden cast, whilst the large bases were cast from concrete on site. Here concrete would have been poured into wooden shuttering - the outline of the wood can be seen in the concrete. As this base hardened, the cap would have been placed on top.

The purpose of such anti-tank blocks was to obstruct the progress of a tank or other vehicle, or should it attempt to cross them to exposure its vulnerable underneath to the defenders weapons.

Period wartime photographs show that anti-tank blocks of this design were strewn across the beaches at Hastings, having been cast in line after line.

> Access: By foot on Beeding Bridge in The Street over the River Arun.
> Map reference: TQ 193106.

*Above: On this road bridge over the River Adur at Bramber, can be found a remarkably well preserved set of black out markings. In fact the same pattern cane be seen on each corner of the bridges brickwork.*

Not every measure introduced as a result of the black-out imposed by the Emergency Powers Act of May 1940, was a backward step. For the first time ever those riding bicycles at night were compelled to carry and show a rear facing red light. White lines appeared along the centre of roads, something which had been extremely rare before the outbreak of war. Central white lines were just one use for the white paint - curb stones were painted white, as were often the bumpers and running boards of cars. At first only sidelights were permitted, but this was soon relaxed in favour off an obscure offside headlamp, followed by the headlamp cover with horizontal slits in 1940. In the early days of the blackout there had been carnage on British roads, with accidents involving pedestrians and vehicles soaring. In an effort to make things safer for the motorist anything that may have been an obstacle was painted with vertical or horizontal black and white lines - such as above. Another example can be seen at <u>Borde Hill</u>, on the corners of Skew Bridge, Borde Hill Lane, TQ 325274.

*Above: Another example of black-out markings can be seen on the walls of this pillbox that once stood at the end of Sea Lane in Rustington. The road here bends through almost 90 degrees, and so to give drivers making their way at night with only faint light from the covered headlamps, such markings would have been painted all over the sides of this pillbox, (Photograph reproduced by the kind permission of Mrs M. Taylor). Left: Yet another example of such markings, this time on a gatepost at the junction of Shripney Lane and the A29 Shripney Road, Bognor Regis.*

# COLDWALTHAM
## PRISONER-OF-WAR CAMP

*Access: By foot along public footpath from the end of Church Lane.*
*Map reference: TQ 023167.*

*Left: Though still standing, this remaining accommodation hut is slowly being overtaken by modern development - note the new foundations in the foreground. It is believed that further remains of this camp can be found on private land located behind this building.*

Only a few facts are known of this Prisoner-Of-War camp that can be found alongside the public footpath that leads from Church Lane. It is believed that the huts were originally built to accommodate British and Canadian Troops, but that as the war progressed the influx of German and Italian prisoners became critical. Indeed, local people believe that it was Italian prisoners who were accommodated here from 1942 onwards. As time passed, the Italians were permitted more and more freedom, so much so that they were eventually able to leave the camp during the day to work in the surrounding area - in particular on local farms. In fact, local history has it that security at the camp became so lax  the prisoners would often sneak out at night, returning just in time for the morning roll-call!!.

107

# WESTHAMPNETT
## PARACHUTE STORE

> Access: On foot at the entrance to the Goodwood Motor Circuit.
> Map reference: SU 879075.

*Above: One of the many surviving wartime buildings at Westhampnett airfield is this parachute store. It can be found just beyond the current entrance to Goodwood Motor Racing Circuit off Claypit Lane. It is believed that this is the only surviving parachute store on any of the former wartime airfields in Sussex.*

Prior to the expansion programme of the late 1930s, parachute stores on RAF airfields were commonly found to be adaptations of an existing building, with the results often being far from satisfactory.

A standard design was drawn up, of which this parachute store at Westhampnett is an example. Proper hanging, folding and storage space was provided. Wartime shortages meant that a cheap, easily constructed building was required, and with this thought in mind the designers used the commercially available Maycrete Hut, with its external wall supports, as the basis.

The centre roof was raised to a higher level to allow room to hang drying parachutes, whilst the whole building was glazed and ventilated with an efficient heating system to maintain an even temperature and reduce condensation to a minimum.

> Access: On foot in layby at the side of the A283, Stopham Road.
> Map reference: TQ 054183.

*Above: Lying in a lay-by alongside the A283 Stopham Road in Stopham is this memorial to a local rector killed just after the Battle of Britain. The inscription reads: "Near this spot William Beech Masefield (Late Chaplin R.N.), for seven years rector of the parishes of Stopham and Hardham, was killed by enemy action, October 4th 1940".*

William Masefield was the only person to die as the result of enemy action in either Stopham or Hardham. It appears that on the 4th of October 1940, where records show some eight high explosive bombs were dropped on the parish, Masefield had set out on his bicycle along the Stopham Road to visit some ill parishioners. As he cycled along he became the victim of a single German bomber as it ditched its cargo of 8 bombs across the road. Masefield was killed instantly, and one other person was injured in this air-raid.

This was the first of three air-raids that took place over Stopham. The next occurred two years later on the 18th May 1942, when some 4 high explosive bombs were dropped. On this occasion no one was killed or injured. The final attack took place on the 24th February 1944, when an unknown number of incendiaries fell on the parish, again with no injuries or loss of life.

# PARHAM
## STRAWBERRY GROVE ARMY CAMP

*Location: In the private grounds of the Saw Mill, Parham House.*
*Map reference: TQ 063153.*

*Above: The rusting remains of a line of Nissen Huts is all that survives to mark the location of Strawberry Grove camp, which is now an operational sawmill within the grounds of Parham Estate. The shells of some 6 Nissen huts can still be found here.*

As already mentioned in this book, the influx of large numbers of British and Canadian troops into Sussex saw army camps being constructed where ever possible. The grounds of Parham Estate provided the open space required, and in fact the estate records show that the Canadian Engineers which arrived in the Summer of 1942 constructed three camps in the grounds. These were called the East Park Wall camp; the Windmill Hill camp; and the Strawberry Grove camp.

From 1942 to 1943 Strawberry Grove camp was occupied by the men of the 16th Field Company Royal Canadian Engineers, and then from Autumn 1943 to April 1944 by the 2nd Field Company. Following the departure of the Canadians, on the 18th April 1944 the 15th Scottish Division Engineers moved in, with the 279 Field Company Royal Engineers the occupiers of Strawberry Grove Camp. Eventually the camp was inhabited by students of the Canadian School of Infantry up until time the camp was turned over to the control of the estate authorities in 1947.

# NEWHAVEN
## CAPONNIERE STEPS (WITH A NASTY SURPRISE)

Location: Entrance in grounds of Newhaven Fort, Newhaven.
Map reference: TQ 448002.

*Above: These steps that lead from the main area of the Fort down to the Caponniere at the base of cliffs are hard work on the way down, let alone on the way back up!. (Photographed by kind permission of the Director of Newhaven Fort).*

The reason for the inclusion of this site in this book is by virtue of its wartime role within the day to day operation of Newhaven Fort. The steps are the only method of access from the main area of the fort down to the defensive caponniere which is located at the base of the cliffs below the Fort.

Having decided that the steps may have provided an easy method of entry into the Fort by any attacking German troops, the wartime British occupiers of the Fort came up with an interesting and somewhat fearsome method of defence!. A large drum of petrol was kept at the top of the steps to be poured down at the storming troops. The petrol would then have been ignited by a grenade, engulfing the attackers in an inferno from which they would have had difficulty escaping.

# HAILSHAM
## BURTON WALK

Access: By foot in Burton Walk at the junction with Lindfield Drive.
Map reference: TQ 588092.

*Above: This road sign in Hailsham is a fitting memorial to Flying Officer Percey Burton, who died during the Battle of Britain on 27th September 1940 following aerial combat with a Messerschmitt Bf-110.*

Percey Burton was a 21 year old South African who, like many of his compatriots, had travelled to Britain to join the Royal Air Force on the outset of the Second World War. At the time of the crash he had been flying a Hurricane Fighter, number V6559, of 249 Squadron based at North Weald airfield.

That morning the German attack had begun early but nevertheless the RAF Fighter Squadrons rose to the attack. Burton latched onto one particular Bf-110 which was, unfortunately for him, piloted by a very experienced pilot - Horst Liensberger, the Gruppe Kommandeur of V/LG1. Burton chased the Bf-110, often at tree top height, until when above Hamlins Mill in Hailsham both aircraft lurched upwards. The Bf-110 fell to the ground in Simmons Field, whilst at 9.50am the Hurricane of Percey Burton crashed near Station Road in Hailsham. Burton was killed instantly as were the German crew. From the wreckage it is believed that having run out of ammunition, and determined not to let the Germans escape, Burton rammed the Bf-110.

# FORD
## BLISTER HANGER

Location: On agricultural land north of Horsemere Green Lane, Ford.
Map reference: SU 994024.

*Above: One of the three surviving blister hangers that still remain on or around the now disused airfield at Ford. Modern adaptations have seen the ends of the hanger closed off with a mixture of brick and corrugated steel sheeting. This hanger can be found at the south end of the airfield near the end of the Southwest to Northeast runway. Every Sunday Ford airfield is home to a Sunday Market, allowing one access to the remains of both of the airfields wartime runways.*

The airfield at Ford was first established in 1918 as part of an American Air Force deal with the British aircraft manufacturers Handley Page. The Americans had agreed to purchase Handley Page bombers if the British company provided five fully equipped airfields. The sites chosen were Tangmere, Rustington, Emsworth, Goring and of course Ford. After the end of the First World War, Ford reverted back to agriculture. In 1938, the massive expansion programme of the RAF saw Ford being once again requisitioned.

Ford is interesting in that many of the wartime buildings still remain, particularly in the area now occupied by Ford Prison. The Prison occupies many of the original administration buildings that can be found off Church Lane. By the end of the Second World War Ford had 5 Bellman hangers, 1 general-purpose hanger and 4 blister hangers. Of the latter, (an example of which is above), it is believed that three still remain. One can be found on the southern airfield perimeter (above), one on the north side beyond Ford Lane, and the last within the grounds of the Prison. Much of the two concrete runways still remain, though in parts these have had grain stores and even a factory built on them.

113

# SELSEY
## BISMARK VICTIM'S MEMORIAL

*Access: At the front of Selsey Church on the B2145, Chichester Road.*
*Map reference: SZ 855937.*

*Above: At the front of Selsey Church in Chichester Road, Selsey, is the village war memorial. On the memorial is the name of Frederick Roy Fullick, who died on the 24th May 1941 - a victim of the German Battleship 'Bismark'.*

Frederick Roy Fullick was born in Selsey on the 7th March 1921, and on completing school immediately entered the Royal Navy. Initially starting as a 'boy sailor', he was later in his service posted onto the British Battlecruiser H.M.S. Hood. At the same time it is believed that he was promoted to Able-Seaman.

On the 24th May 1941 the 'Hood' sighted the 'Bismark' in the Atlantic between Iceland and Greenland in the Denmark Strait. Along with H.M.S. Prince of Wales, the 'Hood' opened fire, but mistaking the 'Prinz Eugen' for the Bismark. The 'Bismark' replied immediately hitting the 'Hood'. So bad was the damage that at 0600 the 'Hood' suffered a huge explosion, split in two and sank. Almost all of the 1,300 crew on the 'Hood' died, including AB Fullick, who died at the tender age of just 20.

# HORSHAM
## ROYAL OBSERVER CORPS CENTRE

*Location: In the grounds of the Territorial Army Barracks, Denne Road.*
*Map reference: TQ 173303.*

*Above: The Royal Observer Corps Centre at Horsham. On the right hand side is the cooling tower, whilst in the middle of the facing wall are the main entrance doors. The tower in the background is part of the modern military barracks.*

This building located at the rear of the military barracks in Denne Road was the headquarters of number 2 Group (Horsham) of the Royal Observer Corps. It is at this centre that the plots and reports from all the outlying Observer Posts would arrive, be processed and then passed on to the various RAF commands and central processing centres such as that at Bletchley Park which throughout the war was the home of the commanders of Britain's air defence.

One Horsham woman, Mrs Nellie Gill, remembers her service in the centre, having been given a choice of service in the land-army, a munitions factory or in the Observer Corps. She was given six weeks initial training, issued her uniform (which included one skirt and enough material to make a second) and set to work on the plotting tables. She remembers working a three shift pattern, with each shift consisting of some eight hours.

*Left: The main entrance into the centre. Protected by a pair of enormous steel, air tight doors, entry was gained by using the phone mounted on the wall - the yellow box on the left. Below: The scene on the inside of the centre after the installation of the long-range board which is where the controllers in the foreground are working. On the main table are being plotted Mustangs, Spitfires and a variety of bombers, (Photograph by kind permission of Mr D. Wood).*

*Left: A mock-up of the inside of a R.O.C Centre such as at Horsham. This can in fact be seen within the Royal Observer Corps display at Newhaven Fort. It is likely that there would have been more controllers, all of whom were given the status of special constables during their service, (Photographed by kind permission of the Director of Newhaven Fort).*

*Right: An exterior view of the air conditioning tower - note the large protected vents on each side of the tower. At the time of going to press it was rumoured that the ROC Centre at Horsham was going to be demolished in order to make way for an expansion of the barracks.*

# AMBERLEY
## BRITISH 2" MORTAR BOMB

> Location: In private agricultural land south of the South Downs Way.
> Map reference: TQ 047128.

*Above: Shown exactly as found - the spent remains of a British 2" mortar bomb. It may see[m] incredible that so many years after the war. this was only one of about 8 of these mortar bombs th[at] were all found in the same field on the side of the South Downs. None were buried, but simply lying [on] top of the grass.*

The British 2" mortar was a smooth bore, muzzle loaded weapon with a high angle of fire. [It] could be carried into action by a single soldier, had a range of some 470 yards, weighed 23. pounds and produced a rate of fire of 5 rounds per minute. The 2" mortar bomb shown her[e] was found to be a spent smoke bomb, as were all the mortar bomb remains in this fiel[d]. However, the determination of this fact was left to the professionals - the finder of thes[e] remains took the wise precaution of staying clear and calling in the Army Bomb Dispos[al] Unit.

It is worth noting that nearby on top of the Downs, around a small copse, were found [a] number of 2" mortar bomb fuse caps. It is likely that the mortar bombs were fired, by [a] soldier, from here onto the hillside in support of his colleagues who were no doubt o[n] exercise at the time.

> Access: By foot in the grounds of Tangmere Church, Church Lane.
> Map reference: SZ 903063.

*Left: In a quiet corner of the Churchyard at St. Andrews Church, Tangmere is the grave of another young RAF pilot. Sgt. Ben Bingley was only 24 years old when he died at the controls of his Spitfire on the 10th March 1941. The plane, from 616 Squadron, was seen to smash into the ground through unexplained reasons at Wiston, near Steyning. Before joining the RAF Bingley had been a hospital administrator at Leicester and, despite this, the decision was made to lay him to rest at Tangmere.*

*Right: Ben Bingley. It is believed that oxygen failure was the most likely cause of his death. His C/O wrote: "They were crossing the coast near Worthing at about 21,000ft when the section leader saw him lagging a long way behind. Shortly after he went into a steep dive and carried on until he hit the ground". (By kind permission of Mr A. Saunders).*

# SHOREHAM-BY-SEA
## NICOLSON DRIVE

> Access: By foot in Nicolson Drive at junction with Buckingham Road.
> Map reference: TQ 218057.

*Above: This road sign stands as a memorial to one of the most famous of the Battle of Britain fighter Pilots. The inscription on the plaque reads: "This road is named in memory of Wing Commander J.B. Nicolson V.C. D.F.C., the only fighter pilot to be awarded the Victoria Cross in World War 2 - killed 2nd May 1945. We will remember them".*

Twenty-one VCs were awarded to the RAF in the Second World War, but only was ever awarded to a fighter pilot during the Battle of Britain. Nicolson had joined the RAF in December 1936, and was serving with No. 72 Squadron at the outbreak of war. He  was posted to No. 249 Squadron at Church Fenton in May 1940, and then as 'A' Flight commander moved south with the Squadron to Boscombe Down on the 14th August 1940.

On the 16th of August 1940, Flight lieutenant James B. Nicolson was leading red section of No. 249 Squadron. An attack by enemy aircraft whilst over Southampton left Nicolson wounded and his Hurricane on fire. When about to bale out, and with flames licking in and around the cockpit, he sighted and shot down one of the attacking aircraft. Only then did he abandon his aircraft. For this act, on the 24th November 1940, Nicolson was invested with the Victoria Cross by King George VI at Buckingham Palace.

Sadly, Nicolson was not to survive to see the peace he had fought for. On the 2nd May 1945, just days before VE-day, he was killed when the No. 355 Squadron Liberator in which he was a passenger crashed into the sea of Calcutta. He died aged just 29.

# CHURCH NORTON
## PETROLEUM WARFARE TANKS

Location: In private woodland adjacent to footpath from Church Norton.
Map reference: SZ 873956.

*Right: The first of four of these concrete underground stores or tanks that can be found in the woodland near the Church car park at Church Norton. All of the tanks have the same style of construction and are joined by a series of pipes covered with blue asbestos.*

These tanks hidden in the woods at Church Norton have been the source of much speculation and puzzlement as to the reason for their existence. Taking all the factors into account the favoured opinion is that they formed the basis of Petroleum Beach Defences. The theory behind this most basic of defences was that thousands of gallons of fuel would be pumped onto a beach, road or wherever the enemy made a landing or appearance. Once discharged the fuel would be set alight, catching the unsuspecting enemy in an instant inferno. It is believed that these four semi-buried tanks were the fuel stores, and that the remains of the small building acted as the control room for the pumping of the fuel out onto the wide, flat, open beaches of Church Norton nearby.

Petroleum warfare was not a new concept for Sussex. From 1940 onwards the buildings of what is now Windlesham School, (on the A24 north of Worthing), were home to the School of Petroleum warfare. One person who remembers the activity at Windlesham is Geoff Goatcher. He states that "the structures at Windlesham were not built for any defensive function, but were directly used for tests at the Department of Petroleum Warfare. The bathroom window of my father's house looked straight across at Windlesham School and Highden Hill. I can remember, as a schoolboy, observing the flame-throwers in action around these structures. I also seem to remember that Highden Clump (a smaller version of Chanctonbury Ring) was destroyed in the course of these activities".

Geoff Goatcher is not the only person to remember the activities of the Department of Petroleum Warfare in Sussex. Alan Shaw was sent to Sussex as Officer in Charge of No.2 Section, 222 Field Company Royal Engineers. "One day I was deputed to attend a demonstration on chalk downland near Brighton of a Petroleum Warfare Department anti-aircraft flame thrower! This took the form of the biggest petrol tanker I had ever seen on which was mounted a 'gun'. This was basically a high-pressure jet able to be directed through a wide arc from the horizontal to the vertical. Thanks to a compressor that was driven by an 850hp Napier Lion aero engine mounted on a trailer behind the tanker, the 'gun' could project a fearsome jet of flame 200 to 300 ft into the air. To add colour to the demonstration, a little Tiger Moth biplane of the RAF was forced to circle nervously above us – taking extreme care not to come within range!"

*Below: The remains of what is believed to have been the control hut for the operation of the flame defences and the storage tanks. Here can be seen the large steel door lying in front of a pile of concrete bricks and parts of the original steel frame in which the door would have been mounted.*

Location: On private agricultural land adjacent to Poling Street.
Map reference: TQ 045052.

*Above: The most obvious remaining feature of the Poling radar station - the receiver block. Minus its blast walls, this building has survived in use as a combined garage and workshop. The brickwork around the top holds in a layer of gravel - used as protection against bomb blasts and shrapnel. Note the drain holes a third of the way down the side of the building which are intended to allow rainwater to drain from this gravel bed.*

One of the first 20 Chain Home radar stations planned before the war, RAF Poling had yet to be completed when the hostilities began, though all was nearly complete by the start of the Battle of Britain.

Originally Poling had four transmitter towers with provision for three 'curtain arrays' of aerials to be slung between them. These towers stood in an east-west line on the most westerly part of the site. Later in the war, one of these towers was removed, with the others remaining till the site was closed down in the mid-1950s. The receiver block shown above was close to the base of these masts.

Poling was also equipped with an underground buried reserve, which was located about 300 yards south of the site boarding Poling Village. When the site was returned to agricultural use, this reserve was collapsed and provided a useful repository for much of the concrete rubble this clearance produced.

*Above: A view of the three large transmitter towers that once stood at Poling. They are not aerials in themselves, but actually have the aerial array slung between them, (By kind permission of Mrs M. Taylor). Left: Very little remains of what once stood on this site. Whilst this structure may have an agricultural appearance it is in fact a standard design air ministry water tower, though more commonly to be found on Britain's airfields.*

> Access: By foot in Bognor Regis Cemetery, off Hawthorn Road.
> Map reference: SZ 931998.

*Above: Hidden amongst the other grave stones in Bognor Regis Cemetery is this grave to an unusual victim of wartime circumstances - William Avis. This is plot 373 AC Con.New. William Avis was buried here on the 3rd March 1942.*

It was dark and late at night on the 26th February 1942, when 47 year old Police Sgt. William Avis, began chasing a Canadian Army soldier who had deserted from his unit, the Royal Canadian Highland Light Infantry. The soldier found himself trapped in Fernhurst Gardens, Bognor Regis, and so in an effort to escape, the deranged deserter, Private John Moore, stabbed Sgt Avis. Avis died that night as a result of these injuries.

On the 28th February 1942, Private Moore was brought back to Chichester Police Station handcuffed to Det. Sgt. Heslin and P.C. Fuller. Here he was charged with the murder of Sgt. Avis and committed for trial at the Old Bailey. In these proceedings, Moore was seen to be clearly unbalanced, insane and therefore not fit for trial. Avis was laid to rest in Bognor Regis Cemetery on the 3rd March 1942.

It is worth noting that on the wall inside the reception area of <u>Chichester</u> Police Station is a wooden carved memorial to those police officers who gave their lives whilst on active service.

# EAST LAVANT
## POLISH AIRMANS CHAPEL

> Location: In the grounds of a private residence off Fordwater Road.
> Map reference: SU 865079.

*Left: This is an example of a somewhat altered Nissen Hut. Once part of the original airfield buildings at the north-west corner of Westhampnett, it is believed that this Nissen hut was changed when the area was used to house Polish refugees. The current owner has always believed that the wife of a Polish chaplain took it on herself to turn this Nissen hut into a place of worship, both for the Polish refugees and Polish Airmen stationed on the airfield.*

It is surprising how much of the original buildings from the wartime airfield at Westhampnett still survive - many hidden in the corner of private houses surrounding the former fighter base.

In the garden of one house in East Lavant alone, it is possible to find the overgrown remains of the Nissen hut shown above, a wash house, part of the airfield's concrete roadways and even a ivy-clad air ministry pattern water-tower!. The present occupier of this land states that towards the end of the war and after, the huts and buildings on this north-west corner of the airfield were occupied by Polish refugees, and that the Nissen hut above was turned into a chapel by the wife of a Polish Chaplain.

> Access: By foot along clifftop at Peacehaven Heights.
> Map reference: TQ 432003.

*Above: The front of the radar station on the cliffs at Peacehaven. The cliff edge is only inches away on the right hand side of this photograph!. The building on which the radar aerial was actually mounted is the structure at the rear, whilst in the foreground is part of the main observation area.*

This radar site was built on the cliffs at Peacehaven, and its sole purpose was to provide the artillery guns of Newhaven Fort and the three emergency coastal batteries near the Fort with their target and range information. From here, the radar operators would monitor and plot the approach of any enemy vessels. The site is completely self contained. At the cliff edge is the building on which the actual radar equipment was mounted and a large observation room. Between these two was the control building for the radar. Towards the rear of the compound were three other buildings - a generator hut, a communications building and a third structure which seems to be a gun store. The information received by the radar would be passed to the guns they controlled by secure telephone lines, or in cases of emergency by radio. Further back up the cliffs are a number of 3.7" light anti-aircraft emplacements which would have defended the radar site when under aerial attack.

*Above: A view of the rear of the main site buildings. On the left is the structure on which the radar itself was mounted - note the radar fitting in the centre of the roof, in the middle the radar control room and on the right the observation room with a large embrasure looking out over the Channel. Below: This building can be found at the rear of the site - and appears to have been either a gun store or general mess room.*

*Above: The communications building. The risk of aerial attack ensured that all the buildings on the site were solidly built. Also of interest is the concrete ramp - an example of which can be seen leading into all the buildings on the site. The ribbing is to assist with grip when moving heavy objects in and out. Right: Inside the communications hut. In the far corner can be seen the wooden tunnelling through which the cables would have passed to the telegraph poles and radio aerials.*

*Above: Of the same design as the communications building is this the generator hut. As is the case throughout the site, this building has been sunk into the ground to aid in its protection. Left: For whatever reason, this is the only building that has not been stripped out inside - the generator, control board, fuses and switchgear are still all present. Whether this is the original equipment fitted is not known.*

> Access: By foot in Bognor Regis Cemetery, off Hawthorn Road.
> Map reference: SZ 930998.

*Right: A victim of a devastating air-raid on Bognor Regis on the 11th of April 1941. Albert Harry Holloway is buried in the same cemetery as the Bognor Police Officer, William Avis, who was killed by a Canadian Army deserter.*

Albert Harry Holloway was 51 years old when he was killed by falling German bombs on the night of the 11th April 1941. Not only was he a Corporal in the Bognor Regis Home Guard, but also spent his time serving as a Firewatcher. He lived at number 34 Havelock Road with his wife K.E. Holloway. It is not known whether Albert Holloway was on duty at the time of his death, in either the Home Guard or ARP capacity, but it is thought that he was killed by an exploding bomb in Havelock Road.

In 1941, Bognor Regis was to suffer some 441 alerts. 86 high explosive, 200 incendiaries and 7 parachute mines were dropped, leaving some 8 people dead and 22 injured.

*Above: A view of the damage that was caused by the German bombers on the 11th April 1941. This i̇*
*Annadale Avenue which caught one of the 24 odd bombs dropped that night in a line from*
*Hillsborough Road to London Road, (Photograph by the kind permission of Mr A. Saunders).*

Access: By foot along public footpath north in Stocks Lane.
Map reference: SU 870075.

*Right: Standing on the western side of the airfield is this example of a Quadrant Tower. On the otherside of the hedge behind the tower is part of the old airfield perimeter, (By kind permission of Dr. M. Osborne).*

It is unusual to find a Quadrant tower like this on what was once a serving fighter base. The main purpose of Quadrant towers was in bombing practice. The tower would have been built alongside the target area or range and would have monitored the approach, angles and accuracy of the bomber carrying out its run. For this reason, no one is certain why such a structure can be found at Westhampnett. It maybe that training of some description was carried out across this airfield or, more likely, that someone needed a building of this design or type for another purpose.

> Access: By foot on the west side of St. Peters Church, Twineham.
> Map reference: TQ 253199.

*Left: In a secluded corner of St Peters Churchyard, Twineham, is this somewhat unique carved wooden memorial to a pilot shot down in an earlier World War.*

This unique gravestone was erected to the memory of one Captain H.E. Comber-Taylor, who whilst serving with the RAF was shot down over the trenches of the western front in 1917 His body was brought back to the family home and buried in their local church here at Twineham.

On the wall of St. Marys Church, Storrington, can be found a large marble memorial to another First World war pilot. Captain Francis Mond had transferred from the Royal Field Artillery to the Royal Air Force, joining 57 Squadron. At the age of 22, on the 15th may 1918, he was killed flying over Bouzencourt on the Somme, whilst fighting several German aeroplanes.

# UPPER DICKER
## CANADIAN WALL ART

Location: In the upper floors of the gatehouse at Michelham Priory.
Map reference: TQ 557094.

*Right: This piece of wall art is believed to have been created by a Canadian Officer during the time he was billeted at Michelham Priory. The question does beg to be asked as to why the actual target area for the D-Day landings should come to be drawn on a gatehouse wall in Sussex!. This could hardly be classed as the best method in which to store such highly classified information - unless, of course, the artist had set to work after the 6th June 1944!, (Photographed by kind of the Director of Michelham Priory and the Sussex Archaeological Society).*

Throughout the pillboxes, emplacements and billets of the Second World War pencilled, painted or scratched notes can be found on the white-washed walls. Examples of this graffiti can be seen at these locations, (amongst others):

Washington. In the loft of Windlesham House, once the home of the Canadian School of Infantry, are poems and names left by Canadian Troops.

Henfield. On pillbox at TQ 211183, the inscription 'Ringmer Building Works, 1940'.

Ardingly. On pillbox at TQ 344273 is written '6986174 Pte Reid TA, Leicester, 1943'

Roman Woods. In this pillbox by the A283, TQ 116333, are both poems and names.

Mannings Heath. At TQ 206294 is a Type 24 pillbox once occupied by Canadian Troops.

*Above: Not the only wartime graffiti to be found in the gatehouse - at the extreme limit of the spiral staircase, in the roof, can be seen these etchings from two troops of 55 Division Signals, left in August 1941. T. Ferguson and Bill Riding were not the only ones to leave reminders of their time at Michelham Priory as the whole wall in this part of the building is covered in pencil scribblings.*

*Left: The gatehouse at Michelham Priory in which both sets of 'graffiti' can be found, though on different floors. (Both photographed by the kind permission of the Director of Michelham Priory and the Sussex Archaeological Society).*

# TANGMERE

## AIR TRAFFIC CONTROL TOWER

> Location: On the northside of the disused airfield at Tangmere.
> Map reference: SU 913066.

*Above: Standing exposed and somewhat hollow-eyed is the old wartime control tower, built after the Battle of Britain, at Tangmere airfield. The control tower lies on the northern perimeter of this now disused airfield, (By kind permission of the West Sussex Gazette, photograph number C9057-1).*

Wartime control towers, or watch offices to use the correct RAF terminology before the transatlantic term took over, come in a variety of shapes and sizes, though the basic box shape was standard. On the rear and one side would be found entrances and an external staircase on one side. To assist in the black-out, many of the windows were often small, though this does not appear to be the case here at Tangmere. Most control towers were two storey, with a glass house added on the roof to improve the view of an airfield. Here at Tangmere the roof has had a purpose built observation room added, and the remainder of the roof space turned into a viewing platform.

The tower's rooms would have been occupied by control, met and teleprinter staff. If the base was a training establishment, then the Chief Flying Instructor would also have had an office in the tower.

At Westhampnett, another surviving wartime control tower can be seen, (SU 877073), and which has been kept open as a cafe - well worth a visit!.

> *Access: By foot on slipway to River Adur, off the High Street.*
> *Map reference: TQ 215050.*

*Left: Hundreds of people daily make their way past this example of a wartime 'Hairpin' road-block - one of at least two examples that still remain to be seen in Shoreham. In the background is the High Street, with Church Street leading off it at the rear.*

It was common for stop-lines or defended areas to include permanent and moveable road blocks. This is a 'hairpin' road block which involved bent steel rods, typically made from pieces of old railway track bent over, being slotted into the sockets cut into the road surface. When not in use, the bent rails would often be stored nearby. Some 3,000 of these 'hairpin' roadblocks were made at the nearby Southern Railway Carriage Works which once stood at Lancing. Other examples can be seen at:

Shoreham-By-Sea: On the eastern side of the old Toll Bridge, at TQ 207059.

South Stoke: On the old road bridge over the Arun, (TQ 027102), below the farmhouse.

# TINSLEY GREEN
## ANTI-AIRCRAFT GUN TOWER

Access: By foot along public footpath east from Radford Road.
Map reference: TQ 294394.

*Right: This anti-aircraft gun tower can be seen by talking the public footpath from Radford Road in Tinsley Green near Crawley. It is believed that there are four of these towers in and around the Crawley area. The tower itself is remarkably well preserved (in fact it is believed to a preservation order on it), with access to the gun floor on the top being possible - though only recommended for those with a head for heights. When standing at the top, one thought immediately enters your mind - how did they ever get the gun up there!.*

A climb of some four storeys is required to get you to the top of this structure, though the view you are rewarded with makes the effort well worth while. At the top it is also easy to see the reasoning behind placing a light anti-aircraft gun on the top of such a tall tower - from the gun floor the weapon has a completely uninterrupted field of fire and line of sight. In the floors below are various rooms - such as cartridge and shell stores, rest rooms and even a communications room from which a secure phone line would have linked the tower to its command centre. When this tower was built is not known, but it would almost certainly have been by 1943 when the Blitz was at its peak, and the threat of the V-1 was looming.

*Above: The gun mount itself, only protected by a two foot high concrete ledge - the risk of accidents must have been most disconcerting for the gun crews working up here!. The gun was most likely to have been the 40mm Bofors L40, which by the end of the war was the standard British Light anti-aircraft gun. It would have been bolted onto the central metal mounting plate.*

*Left: The steps that lead from the main staircase, which in itself is precarious, up onto the gun floor. The cut in the concrete roof is not to make it any easier for a crew-member to get up the ladder, but to ensure that when the shells were brought up (carried on the shoulder of the soldier) it could be done safely.*

# WISTON
## 'JANE' MURAL

Location: On the wall of the main library, Wiston House, Wilton Park.
Map reference: TQ 155123.

*Right: Normally hidden behind a large family portrait in the main library at Wiston House is this painting of 'Jane'. 'Jane' started life as the subject of a Daily Mirror cartoon strip, and was portrayed as a featherheaded blonde whose clothing always seemed to be rationed!. This rendering of Jane is believed to have been painted by one of the many Canadian Officers who were billeted at Wiston House from 1942 onwards. In the summer of 1940 Wiston House became the headquarters of General Bernard Montgomery whilst he prepared his plans for the defence of Britain in the event of a German invasion.; in 1942 the Officers of the Canadian 1st, 2nd and 3rd Army Division, and in particular those of the Light Infantry Regiments. It is unfortunate that this mural, and its remarkably bright colours, is usually hidden from public view, (Photographed by kind permission of Mr J. Melser, General manager, Wiston House).*

The house at Wiston is not only famous for once being the headquarters of General Montgomery, but is also the location of Wilton Park.

Wilton Park is an institution which has performed vital work immediately after the Second World War, and which used to be located near Beaconsfield. It was founded by Professor Sir Heinz Koeppler who had been a senior figure in the wartime Intelligence Services. Starting with senior German Prisoners-Of-War in 1946, and uptil 1950, Wilton Park received those who had lived for so long in a fascist state, and began installing in them an understanding of the workings of democracy. During this period some 4,500 Germans passed through Wilton Park which, by the fact that many went on to become senior West German Politicians, had played an important role in the construction of the democracy of West Germany.

# PAGHAM
## MULBERRY HARBOUR REMAINS

Location: Lying in 9 metres of water, 2 miles out from Pagham Beach.
Reference: 50 44 38; 00 42 19!!.

*Above: This unfortunately poor quality photograph shows a diver on the wreck of a Mulberry harbour which lies in about 9 metres of water some 2 miles out from the beach at Pagham, (By kind permission of Mr K. McDonald and taken from 'Dive Sussex' by Kendall McDonald, published by Underwater World Publications).*

The construction of the Mulberry Units was begun in 1943, though the concrete caissons used were given another, different, code-name - they were called 'Phoenix' units. Some 26 sites were used to build these Mulberry harbours, including locations on the Thames, at Southampton, Portsmouth, Goole, Middlesborough and even Bromborough. The design of the Phoenix units came under the control of the War Office, but once floated off the building site they came under the domain of the Admiralty. They were stored by being sunk and rested on the seabed, with the main parking area for nearly all of the 80 units being off Selsey and Bognor Regis.

One unit, however, was never to make it across to Normandy, and is specifically mentioned in the records. It had been sitting in deep water with no problem, but on the day it came to be moved it was raised to the surface and, due to a lack of tugs, got out of control. She was immediately flooded again, but settled across a depression on the seabed. This caused the structure to twist by as much as 2ft 6", and thus be wrecked beyond repair. This Mulberry Unit now forms one of the best diving sites off the South Coast.

142

> Access: On public display in the grounds of Arundel Castle.
> Map reference: TQ 018073.

*Left: Troops pick over the wreckage of a Junkers Ju-88, which crashed at the edge of Swanbourne Lake on the 13th August 1940. Shot down by Tangmere based Hurricanes whilst on route to bomb Farnborough, the plane struck the beech trees on the west side of the lake tearing itself to pieces, (By kind permission of Mr A. Saunders).*

*Right: In 1989, Swanbourne Lake dried, revealing once again evidence of this crash. Amongst the aircraft parts on the lake bottom lay an unexploded 50kg bomb. This was detonated by No. 33 EOD on the 3rd of November. Even later, in 1990, two more bombs were discovered - one 50kg and two 250kg. Having been defused, one of the latter was given to Arundel Castle, and as shown here can be seen in an alcove off the east passage, (Photographed by kind permission of the Trustees of Arundel Castle).*

143

# BISHOPSTONE
## STATION PILLBOX

*Location: On the roof of Bishopstone Railway Station, Bishopstone.*
*Map reference: TV 468998.*

*Left: Bishopstone railway station as it is today. Many would fail to notice the embrasures of the pillbox set around the roof top - facing in three directions; north-west, north-east and south-west. Not only has this pillbox been well disguised, but the position it maintains on this hill overlooking the Tidemills levels, gives it an excellent tactical advantage. Access into the pillbox is made from one of the station offices, though no member of railstaff appears to posses the necessary keys!.*

Generally speaking, the efforts of camouflaging a pillbox or other defence began at the earliest stages. The Home Guard Fieldcraft manual made the following mention of camouflage during the construction of such defences: " Doubtless the shine of the pillbox will later be camouflaged, possibly the spoil in the field and the track will be ploughed under, but what is the good of doing all this long after the vital information has already been given?. Camouflage is not something to be added at a later date - it is a discipline to be kept from the very moment you start on such works". Worthwhile as it is, this advise is something the builders of this pillbox probably escaped - building a brick structure on top of another.

# TANGMERE
## PICKETT-HAMILTON FORT

Location: On public display in grounds of Tangmere Aviation Museum.
Map reference: SU 906060.

*Right: The Pickett-Hamilton Fort on public display at Tangmere Aviation Museum - the camouflage is a recent addition!. Tangmere was not the original home of the fort, for it was discovered by Royal Engineers as they searched the disused airfield at Merston for pipe-mines laid in the event of an invasion. The ten-ton concrete and metal structure was lifted in two sections and transported to Tangmere for restoration. These forts were placed on most airfields, but in many cases their excellent concealment has meant that many were and still remain undiscovered, (Photographed by kind permission of Director of Tangmere Aviation Museum).*

Officially known as the Pickett-Hamilton Fort, (the word Hamilton meaning pressure), they were placed on the majority of airfields in groups of three in late 1940. Manned by three gunners the object of these forts, placed by the side of the runways, was to pop out of the ground and surprise enemy troops should they ever have attacked the airfield in question. At the end of an attack the fort would be lowered back into the ground to await the next attacking wave!. The raising of the fort was achieved by the men (who had entered via a trap door in the roof) pushing up on the roof, a counterweight then taking over to raise the firing slits up above ground level - allowing the troops to open fire with machine-gun or rifle.

# PETWORTH
## BOMBED SCHOOL MEMORIAL

Access: By foot on roadside at the junction of the A283 and the A272.
Map reference: SU 977224.

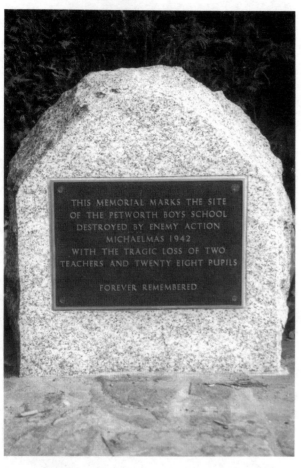

*Left: Standing at the junction of the A283 and A272 is this memorial to the lives of 28 boys and 2 teachers. Resting on the actual site of the destroyed school, the memorial was unveiled during March 1994. It is not the only memorial to this tragic event, for in the Church at Petworth can be found an illustrated manuscript which bears the names of each and everyone of the 30 victims. The inscription on the memorial reads: "This memorial marks the site of the Petworth Boys School destroyed by enemy action Michaelmas 1942 with the tragic loss of two teachers and twenty-eight pupils. Forever remembered".*

It was on the 29th September 1942 that Sussex was to experience one of its worst air-raids. A German bomber unleashed its deadly cargo over Petworth, with the string of bombs falling across the Petworth Boys School. Unfortunately it was day time and the pupils were at school. In the resulting carnage some 28 of the pupils and 2 teachers were killed and the school buildings destroyed, and for many hours the ARP services and Canadian Troops dug into the rubble trying to rescue the victims. Much of this rescue work was carried out by using bare hands. The Canadian Troops had a further role to play when the men of the Canadian Toronto Scottish Regiment formed part of the funeral cortege.

146

> Access: By foot along disused railway line east from Anchor Lane.
> Map reference: TQ 443165.

*Right: The main entrance to this anti-tank pillbox located on the rear wall. Clearly visible is the sheer thickness of these concrete and brick walls - substantial even by today's standards. A doorway this wide was necessary to permit easy access for the artillery piece itself. In the foreground is the embrasure and the square concrete gun mount. Clearly seen is the mounting plate with the eight retaining bolts which would have secured the gun down.*

This anti-tank pillbox is based on the FW 3/28 plans that were drawn up by the Directorate of Fortifications at the beginning of World War 2. This type of pillbox is about 20ft square in size, and has walls at least 3ft thick. This example is unusual in that the embrasure is not wide and short, but is narrow and tall. It is thought that this indicates the pillbox was intended to be used by a 6-pounder artillery piece bolted onto the gun mount. The more usual gun for this type of emplacement was the 2-pounder anti-tank gun, and if sufficient supplies of this weapon had been available then it is likely this pillbox would have been built with the low, wide embrasure.

*Above: A view of the front of this FW 3/28 pillbox. There are many features worthy of note. The first i the staggered and angled edges to the embrasure - this was done to deflect as much incoming fire o shrapnel from entering through the opening into the pillbox. For the same reason, the angled corner were done to increase the structures strength. The pillbox itself has been built facing the disuse railway bridge over the Ouse.*

Such pillboxes generally consist of two chambers; the main one with the entrance for th anti-tank gun, and a smaller one on either side equipped with a number of embrasures which would have been used by defending troops for light machine-gun or rifle fire. A good man examples of these pillboxes exist throughout Sussex, for example:

<u>Bucks Green</u>. Covering the road bridge over the River Arun in Wanford Road, TQ 085327.

<u>Broadbridge Heath</u>. Built alongside Mill Bridge in Wickhurst Lane, TQ 140310.

<u>Ardingly</u>. At TQ 340273, is an example covering Lower Ryelands Bridge, College Road.

<u>Lindfield</u>. The proximity of this pillbox to Buxshalls Bridge on the B2028 at TQ 353263 suggests that the builders had made a mistake.

<u>Lower Horsebridge</u>. At TQ 574112 is an example covering the B2104 bridge over the Ouse.

<u>Barcombe Mills</u>. At TQ 433148 is a bricked up FW 3/28.

# PARHAM
## KITHURST RANGES

> Location: On private agricultural land south of Paygate Cottage, B2139.
> Map reference: TQ 075135.

*Above: The somewhat overgrown remains of the wartime range at Paygate Cottage, Parham, which are locally known as the Kithurst Ranges. The wooden seat supports are still present, though the wood has long rotted away, as are the concrete channels into which the lowered targets would sit.*

There are in fact two ranges at Parham located side by side at the base of the Downs. They date back originally to the Napoleonic Wars, evidenced by the fact that even today musket balls can be found on the site.

It was in 1942 with the arrival of the Canadian Engineers at Parham, that the current shape of the ranges began to be built. The Paygate culvert, known locally as 'target bottom' was rebuilt and a new entrance added. Hard-core for the new concrete butts and range buildings was taken from the rubble that had been placed on the nearby Parham airfield to prevent troops landing. On Friday 5th March 1943 records show that the engineers only had two weeks work left, but that on the 13th May they were still on site!. Once completed, each of the two ranges had eight targets, with range markers at 50, 100, 200, 300 and 400 yards (these can still be seen as ridges in the surrounding field). After the war, the ranges continued in use by the local Air Training Corps and Sussex Police, closing in the early 80s.

149

*Above: The range markers still remain at Kithurst, though it is likely that these are not the original war time examples. Worthy of note is the fact that they are peppered by bullet holes. Equally, the chalk bank in the foreground is a mass of metal - comprising of bent and mangled bullets from 9mm, .303" and 7.62mm rounds!.*

*Left: The eastern end of the butts with the range office disappearing into the undergrowth. It is in this building that the range-keeper would have stored the targets and other equipment.*

# NEWHAVEN
## BATTERY OBSERVATION POST

Location: At the clifftop within the grounds of Newhaven Fort.
Map reference: TQ 448002.

*Above: Yet another of the many wartime structures that can be found on the cliff tops in and around Newhaven Fort is this battery observation post. This is a front view, taken from inside the grounds of the Fort itself, and shows the two separate viewing areas that make up the observation post. A visit to the Fort will enable one to get close up to this structure, with access to both the front and rear, (Photographed by the kind permission of the Director of Newhaven Fort).*

A Battery Observation Post is one of the many buildings that would have existed at a coastal artillery battery. As well as the observation post the batteries may well have had their own defences, for example Bren-gun and spigot mortar posts, anti-aircraft guns, accommodation huts, cook-houses, and almost certainly a guardhouse. However, the layout at Newhaven does not conform to what one would expect of a typical wartime battery by virtue of the fact that it is located on an existing pre-World War One Fort.

As can be seen above, the Battery has two separate viewing galleries, one which would have been to direct the guns themselves, and the other to control and direct the supporting searchlights.

*Above:* *A rear view of the battery observation post. Just visible on the far left of the photograph is the end of the western harbour arm, and which shows the view that the observation and command staff would have had from this structure. Of interest is the small office nearest the camera with the remains of a chimney on the roof - possibly a mess room for the troops manning the post. Right: Another shot of the left hand observation building, the right being buried under this mound. Of interest here is the roof - note the concrete base and securing bolts located in the middle. This may well have been to support a searchlight, (Photographs taken by the kind permission of the Director Of Newhaven Fort).*

# POLING
## MACHINE-GUNNED HOUSE

Location: Private dwelling along track west from Poling Street.
Map reference: TQ 044051.

*Above: The surviving Air Ministry living quarters that can be found on the site of the wartime radar station at Poling. Now private houses, these buildings bear the scars of the various air raids made on the radar station, (By kind permission of Mr A. Oliver).*

If one looks at aerial photographs taken of the radar station whilst still in use, it can clearly be seen that these air ministry houses, intended as living quarters for the NCOs based at the station, had an unhealthy proximity to the large transmitter towers. As a result there is no doubt that they would have suffered when the Germans attempted to knock out the radar equipment. In this photograph can be seen the scars made by bomb splinters and gunfire that occurred in these raids. At the time the damage was repaired by filling the holes with wet concrete - with the result that now the scars are immediately visible.

Whilst in use the radar station provided much mystery for the local people. When the towers first appeared, all manner of fantastic tales were told - how many times were stories told of cars mysteriously brought to a halt when passing Poling Corner!. Equally, many a local farmer was heard to comment "Isn't there any danger of these 'death rays' getting out of control"!.

# STORRINGTON
## CARL DAVIS GRAVE

> Access: By foot in the grounds of St. Marys Church, Church Street.
> Map reference: TQ 086142.

*Left: In Storrington Churchyard is this grave to a Battle of Britain pilot born in South Africa of American parents, but with a love of England. It is unusual that his grave does not have a Commonwealth War · Graves Commission headstone. The grave bears the inscription: "Flt Lieut Carl Raymond Davis DFC, 601 Squadron AAF, Born 30th July 1911, killed in action in the Battle of Britain, 6th September 1940".*

Carl Raymond Davis was born in 1911 in South Africa of American parents, but gained love of England when he was sent to Sherborne School. Having qualified as a minin engineer and married he came to live with the rest of his family in Fryern House, a statel house which once stood in Storrington. Flight Lieutenant Davis is believed to hav accounted for at least 11.5 enemy aircraft, including three in one day, and was awarded th Distinguished Flying Cross.

On the 6th September 1940 he was flying Hurricane P3363 of 601 Squadron from Tangmer when he became involved in a dog-fight over Kent. At about 9.30am he was shot down by Me-109, crashing in the garden of Canterbury Cottage, Matfield. Davis was killed in th crash at the age of 29. He was buried in Storrington Churchyard on the 13th September.

> Access: By foot along track north from Barcombe Mills, north of River.
> Map reference: TQ 438157.

*Above: Painted on the front of the interior blast wall of this Type 22 pillbox is the inscription A247. In fact all the pillboxes in this area carry such a code number. It is usually painted in the same location, and always in ascending or descending order depending upon which way you are heading up or down the Ouse Valley. The next pillbox up the valley, for example, has the code A248, whilst the one immediately south the letters A246.*

Why should this Type 22 anti-infantry pillbox, and all the others of whichever design, in the Ouse valley bear such code numbers. The answer can be reasonably explained by plotting the location of all the pillboxes in the Ouse valley on an old 1" scale map. Do so and you will find a large number of pillboxes in a small geographic area.

It is likely that some enterprising Officer had contemplated the problems that might have risen had he issued orders to his troops, in times of attack, giving the grid reference of the pillbox that each man was to attend. The dense proximity of the pillboxes would have made issuing an identifying grid reference very difficult, with the horrible possibility that all the men from one unit, having mapped out their grid reference, would have tried squeezing into one pillbox. By supplying the troops with a code as well as the grid reference the manning of the pillboxes in a time of haste would no doubt have been a much smoother operation!.

155

> Access: By foot in public carpark at Ditchling Beacon.
> Map reference: TQ 333130.

*Left: A memorial to yet another Battle of Britain Pilot who gave his life defending the British skies. This one can be found on the Sussex Downs above Ditchling. The plaque reads: "Given to the National Trust by Sir Stephen Demitriadi in memory of his son, Flying Officer Richard Stephen Demitriadi, who was killed in action during the Battle of Britain on 11th August 1940, at the age of 21".*

On the 11th of August 1940, the Hurricanes of 601 Squadron took off from Tangmere turned south and headed out to sea climbing to meet the enemy over the Channel. Flying Officer Richard Demetriadi was with them, behind the controls of Hurricane R4092.
At 10.50am, during combat off Portland Bill, Demetriadi was shot down. One of his fellow pilots later commented: "When the boats returned and Richard had not been picked up, hi Squadron Leader and three others flew out to sea to find him. They covered some 30 squar miles, often only 50 feet above sea level, but found no trace of either Richard or his plane. He must therefore have gone down with his plane, suggesting that he had been shot himself".

# LITTLEHAMPTON
## VEHICLE WATERPROOFING TEST SITE

Access: By foot beside Mewsbrook Boating lake and Park, Sea Road.
Map reference: TQ 043015.

*Above: At the south end of the boating lake in Mewsbrook Park is this concrete ramp, now used solely for the launching of pleasure boats. It was back in 1942 that it found a new use!.*

With the threat of a German invasion almost non-existent by 1942, the British and Canadian troops stationed throughout Sussex realised that one day they would be going onto the offensive. Indeed, this offensive was to come sooner that expected, especially for the Canadians, in the form of the Dieppe Raid.
As part of the preparations for a seabourne attack, vast numbers of military vehicles had to be waterproofed. In particular, in the lead upto D-Day the number of vehicles that needed treating was impressive. The actual waterproofing of the vehicles - soft skins, armoured cars and tanks alike, was carried out by the respective motor pool staff, but it was decided that the vehicles needed to be tested rather than experience a failure at the most inopportune moment!. To this end, it is believed that Canadian Engineers adapted the boating lake in Mewsbrook park so that vehicles could drive through in a small loop, putting the waterproofing to test.

*Left: A Daimler Dingo Scout Car enters a purpose built test tank, (By kind permission of the Tank Museum, Bovington). Below: A sketch produced by Mr Glen Bruce shows his recollections of the vehicle waterproofing test site that was adapted from the boating lake in Mewsbrook park. The exit ramp has been removed since the end of the war, (By kind permission of Mr G. Bruce).*

Ramp made in concrete bank.
(Repairs can still be seen).

MEWSBROOK BOATING LAKE.

# WESTERTON
## AIRFIELD SHELTERS

> Location: On private agricultural land in the grounds of Westerton Farm.
> Map reference: SU 888075.

*Right: The eastern entrance to this rectangular shaped shelter. Each side is protected by a triangular shaped blast wall. Inside there are no fixtures or fittings remaining, and the by now expected graffiti adorns the walls.*

Part of the remains of the outbuildings for Westhampnett airfield is this shelter which can be found to the north-east of the airfield. Located on a piece of open farm land, it stands next to a section of pre-cast concrete roadway. Its location some half a mile from the airfield perimeter suggests that whilst having the appearance of an air raid shelter, it is more likely to have been used as an ammunition store. Although I have called it a shelter for the purpose of this book, the fact that both of the entrances are directly opposite each other, suggests that it was not built to have been used as an air raid shelter - having entrances in this manner would have allowed blast from an explosion to rip through the centre of the building. Does anyone know the buildings true purpose?.

> Access: In the corner of the graveyard, Boxgrove Church, Church Lane.
> Map reference: SU 907075.

*Left: William Fiske III lies buried here in the Churchyard at Boxgrove. Once again his grave is not marked by the presence of a Commonwealth War Graves Commission headstone. The inscription on the grave has weathered badly, but reads: "Pilot Officer William Fiske III, Born June 4th 1911 in Chicago. Killed in action Aug 17th 1940. He died for England".*

William Meade Fiske III was a wealthy stockbroker, film producer and international sportsman who hailed from the city of Chicago. Despite the fact that the American authorities frowned upon foreign enlistment, Fiske eventually joined the RAF on the 1st of September 1939 aided by his friends in No. 601 County of London Squadron - also known as the 'Millionaires Squadron'. It was this Squadron that Fiske had joined by the start of the Battle of Britain. During the Battle on the 16th August 1940 Fiske was seriously burnt, so much so that on the 17th he died of his injuries aged 29 years. The death of such a noted society figure caused much publicity, and on the 4th July 1941, American Independence Day, Sir Archibald Sinclair, unveiled a plaque to Fiske in the crypt of St. Pauls Cathedral.

# TREYFORD
## GERMAN PILOTS MEMORIAL

> Access: By foot along public footpath from the Royal Oak, Hooksway.
> Map reference: SU 824171.

*Right: It is unusual to find a memorial to a pilot so far out in the countryside, but this example near Treyford is the more unusual for the fact that it commemorates the death of a German pilot. The flint memorial was erected by the family of the pilot, who travelled to this spot and erected the memorial using Sussex flint they had themselves collected.*

In the furious air battle that took place in the skies over Sussex on the 13th August 1940, three aircraft were to be lost in the Midhurst area - two 43 Squadron Tangmere based Hurricanes, and a Junkers Ju-88. The Junkers was seen to hurtle towards the ground where it exploded in isolated woodland near Treyford. Before it crashed three of the crew were able to bale out, but a fourth failed to escape. This was the pilot, Joseph Oestermann, of whom no trace was ever found. The remainder of his crew were taken into captivity.

All that existed at the crash site that was recognisable were the cylinder liners and a propeller, but nevertheless the local schoolboy population still attended in the hope of finding a souvenir or two.

*Above: The inscription on the memorial, which reads "In memoriam, Hauptmann Joseph Oestermann, Pilot KG54 STAB1, 1915-1940". Below: The wreckage at the crash site. Whilst visiting the memorial the author's girlfriend, waiting for the photography to finish, found some deformed pieces of aluminium. Investigation of the surrounding pathway and undergrowth revealed a large number of small pieces of wreckage. (By the kind permission of Mr A. Saunders).*

# PULBOROUGH
## ROYAL OBSERVER CORPS POST

Location: In field adjacent to public footpath from Mare Hill Road.
Map reference: TQ 061188.

*Above: The badge of the Royal Observer Corps, which would have been worn on the left breast pocket. Right: Some of the few bricks and concrete blocks that remain to remind us of the location of the Pulborough Observer Corps post.*

The Observer Corps post in Pulborough was first opened in 1929, but did not move to the location shown here until April 1939. This position was on top of a hill overlooking Pulborough and the watermeadows of Amberley Wild Brooks below. To the south are the South Downs and the gap in the Downs through which the River Arun passes on its way to the coast at Littlehampton. From this location, the observers would have monitored the passage of aircraft northwards and passed this information to the Command Centre of Number 2 Group at Horsham. In May 1954, the Post 2/0.2 was again to move, and was turned into an underground observer post in June 1968. The Pulborough post was to continue in use until the Observer Corps was decommissioned in 1991.

*Above: This wartime photograph shows the post at Pulborough basking in the summer sunshine during the Battle of Britain, 1940. Note the plotting equipment arranged in the centre of the post, (By kind permission of Mr Derek Wood). Left: Some of the other remains that surround the site of the post. Here some more of the concrete blocks, along with the rusting remains of a seat frame.*

# BURY
## NISSEN HUT

Access: By foot along footpath from Church Lane through Dorset House.
Map reference: TQ 017133.

*Above: This building is an example of what is commonly called a 'Nissen Hut', but is in fact correctly termed as a Curved Asbestos Hut. Asbestos cement provided a cheap and economical building material. Left: A Canadian soldier, Joseph Bernier, photographed on the south coast of England, August 19th 1942. He remembers being stationed in Bury and billeted in Nissen Huts that once existed in the woods at the top of Bury Hill. He also recalls the Canadian guns once arranged in gun-pits near Whiteways Lodge, Bury Hill, (By kind permission of Mr J.A .A. Bernier).*

# WEST DEAN
## PILOT OFFICERS GRAVE

Access: By foot in south west corner West Dean Graveyard, A286.
Map reference: SV 858125.

*Left: At the rear of West Dean Cemetery is this Commonwealth War Graves Commission headstone. It bears the inscription "Pilot Officer J.R.B. Meaker D.F.C, Pilot, Royal Air Force, 27th September 1940, Age 21".*

James Reginald Bryan Meaker had joined the R.A.F before the war and was posted to No. 46 'Uganda' Squadron. Having served in Norway flying Gladiators, he returned to the U.K. on 2nd May 1940 and was posted to No. 240 'Gold Coast' Squadron, flying Hurricanes. In August 1940, the squadron came south to assist in the Battle of Britain. On the 27th September Pilot Officer Meaker D.F.C. was forced to abandon his damaged Hurricane, but in so doing he hit the aircraft's tail plane. He fell thousands of feet to earth, his parachute unopened. He was buried in West Dean Cemetery, his parents also now lying nearby.

> Access: On common land adjacent to Framfield Road, Buxted.
> Map reference: TQ 497234.

*Above: One of at least three wooden framed buildings that exist on this area of common land at Buxted. It is of a design used during the war by the Air Ministry, and is in fact known as an 'Air Ministry Sectional Timber Hut'.*

It is not known why the Air Ministry design huts should be found here at Buxted. However, Sectional Hutting was first introduced in 1935, primarily for those R.A.F posts which were intended to be only temporary. Later they were also used to supplement existing accommodation on older airfields. These huts of which there were a number of different designs had sections that could be bolted together to produce a hut of any length. Each of the sections were individually secured by peg foundations. It was only expected that such huts would have had a lifespan of between 5 and 15 years.

This is not the only remains of a Military establishment in the area. At Maresfield, TQ 463238, there still exists some of the buildings of a once sprawling army camp.

# SADDLESCOMBE
## UNDERGROUND AMMUNITION STORE

*Location: On private land to the north west of the South Downs Way.*
*Map reference: TQ 269117.*

*Left: This almost buried brick structure is almost certainly part of the remains of an old, disused kiln, and can be found in an overgrown quarry near the South Downs Way at Saddlescombe. It is a good example of the type of location utilised by the military throughout the war for the storage of ammunition.*

As D-Day began to approach in late 1943, early 1944, both the R.A.F. and Army began to stockpile vast quantities of ammunition, shells and explosives. The existing storage sites could not cope with such amounts, and as a result the military took to storing its supplies where ever it could. Quiet country lanes, village greens, by-passes, under bridges and even empty barns were used. For example, one of the bridges over which the A23 passes at Slaugham, TQ 264278, was closed and used for the storage of artillery shells. This had the added advantage of the stockpile being hidden from aerial observation. The brick structure shown above, and the surrounding quarry, are another example. Local residents say that Canadian units stationed in the area made use of this location to store ammunition in the lead upto D-Day.

# STORRINGTON
## EXHUMED CHURCHILL TANK

Access: By foot along path from South Downs Way, Springhead Hill.
Map reference: TQ 072122.

*Above: A Mark II Churchill Tank sits in the corner of a field near the South Downs Way, only yards from the grave from which it was recovered. The engine covers lie on the ground in front, whilst behind are the rest of the tracks. On the front of the turret can be seen the faint remains of a blue triangle, which would have indicated that this was a tank belonging to the 'A' Squadron of the Calgary Regiment.*

The 14th Canadian Army Tank Battalion arrived in Britain in late 1940, and were immediately posted to Bordon Camp in Hampshire to begin their basic training. Here they were issued with their first tanks - obsolete French Renault models and a handful of British Matilda tanks. By the middle of 1941 the 14th Canadian Army Tank Battalion, or the Calgary Regiment as it became known, had arrived at Seaford as part of the 2nd Canadian Army Division. Here they learnt that they were to lose their elderly training tanks, and that they were to join the ranks of the armoured units of the Free Polish Army and British Army in being equipped with Mark I Churchill Tanks.

By the start of 1942 the Mark Is had been replaced by between 36 and 38 Mark II Churchills, and as the Regiment was organised along British lines, (See page 171), one of these new Churchills went to the Second troop of 'A' Squadron.

*Above: Despite having been slowly rusting and buried for the last 50 years, these markings on f front of the hull of the Churchill are remarkably well preserved and have proved instrumental discovering the history of the tank. The blue square on the left carries the numbers 175 in white, an indicates the Calgary Regiment, whilst the red and white bands on the right represent the standa British and Canadian armoured fighting vehicle recognition sign used prior to the white star of a the Allied Forces. Below: The shield of the Calgary Regiment.*

# The King's Own Calgary Regiment (RCAC)

*Regimental March:* ‹Colonel Bogey›

*Motto:* ONWARD

# REGIMENTAL HEADQUARTERS
LOCATED AT SEAFORD CAMP, SEAFORD, EAST SUSSEX

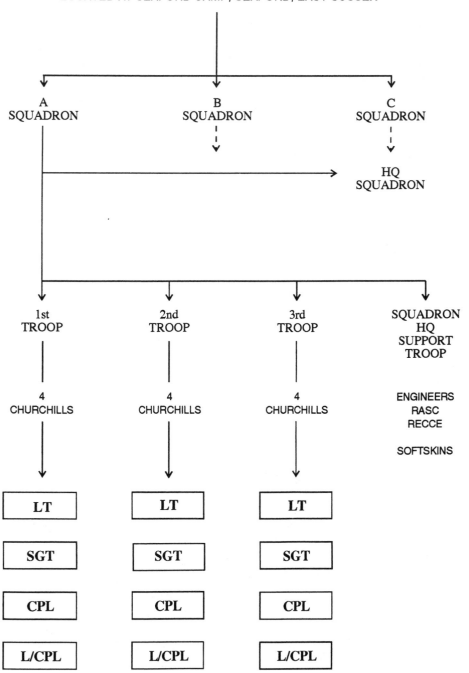

A
SQUADRON

B
SQUADRON

C
SQUADRON

HQ
SQUADRON

1st
TROOP

2nd
TROOP

3rd
TROOP

SQUADRON
HQ
SUPPORT
TROOP

4
CHURCHILLS

4
CHURCHILLS

4
CHURCHILLS

ENGINEERS
RASC
RECCE

SOFTSKINS

| LT | LT | LT |

| SGT | SGT | SGT |

| CPL | CPL | CPL |

| L/CPL | L/CPL | L/CPL |

*Above: When first seen by the author in 1988 almost nothing could be seen of the buried and upside down Churchill. In fact, all that was visible to the human eye is this piece of rusted steel, which is in fact one of the rear offside bogies. Below: A Mark I or Mark II Churchill of the Calgary Regiment the 14th Canadian Army Tank Battalion, on exercise on an area called Tidemills near Seaford. This photograph is believed to have been taken in the winter of 1941 whilst the regiment was based on camp near Seaford Head.*

*Above:* The Churchill being dragged across the field by two Foden wreckers of 118 Recovery *Company, R.E.M.E. (V), Territorial Army.* The hull was placed at the side of the field, and then joined *by its turret and tracks.* On the front of the tank can be seen the two main bogeys, with their rubber *layers still intact after 50 years underground.*

By the 15th May 1942 the Calgary Regiment had received a total of 54 Churchill tanks spread through the nine troops of the three squadrons, as well as the various HQ, Squadron Command Troop and other support units. By now the Regiment was training hard for the forthcoming raid on the port of Dieppe. Much of these exercises took place around the demolished village of Tidemills, near Seaford.

It was during this important training leading upto the Dieppe raid that 'A' Squadron suffered what was then unceremoniously termed a 'dead-head'. This was the serious breakdown of a tank, and it is believed that due to the impending Dieppe raid and the gradual re-supply with Mark IIIs, this 'dead-head' was deemed as unsuitable for repair and withdrawn from service. It was then handed over to the infantry units of the 2nd Canadian Army Division and taken by them to the infantry training grounds above Storrington. Here the tank was used as a range target being fired upon by PIAT anti-tank weapons, amongst others, and when the troops pulled out after the war, was left sitting on the Downs. After the war, a member of the range clearing teams, who now lives in Storrington, remembers that to remove the tank it was simply rolled over into a bomb crater and buried!. On the 20th November 1993, the tank was recovered by the R.E.M.E. having been unearthed over the previous years by a number of hardy enthusiasts. Once rolled out of its grave it was placed on the edge of the field where it remains to this day.

*Above: The author's father, Peter Mace, and Major Anderson from the Tank Museum at Bovington, as they try to free the rear engine covers from the bottom of the hole from which the tank was removed. When the tank was buried immediately after the war by the clearance teams, it was rolled over into a shell crater, coming to rest on its turret. Below: The men of 118 Recovery Company, R.E.M.E (T.A.) lower the turret onto the hull.*

> Access: By foot along the South Downs Way, east from the A24.
> Map reference: TQ 101109.

*Right: Photographed from the South Downs Way are these two barns - the restored remains of the once thriving hamlet of Cobden. Cleared by the army from 1940 onwards Cobden had once been a busy farming hamlet, consisting of a large manor house, cottages, barns and other associated buildings. Once cleared they formed the main target area for the artillery ranges that this area of the South Downs then became, the buildings of Cobden destroyed by these artillery guns. Similar remains can be seen at Tide Mills, near Seaford, TV 461004. Here can be seen the derelict remains of buildings, river workings and even the platforms of the old railway station - all cleared to avoid enemy landing cover. (Photograph with the kind assistance of Mr D.F. Mace).*

It was the emergency regulations introduced from 1939 that enabled the military to move into vast areas of the Sussex countryside. Major A.L. Shaw remembers his service with 222 Field Company, Royal Engineers, at Shoreham in 1941. On arrival his unit was faced with a massive and urgent construction programme, all needing an unlimited source of timber to be used as formwork or shuttering. Using the powers installed by the emergency regulations the military cleared and requisitioned the wooden buildings of the then so-called 'bungalow town' on Shoreham Beach. In this way 222 Field Company was in one stroke able to satisfy the majority of its timber needs by dismantling these wooden structures!.

# SHOREHAM-BY-SEA
## DOME TRAINER

Location: On the north east corner of the airfield at Shoreham.
Map reference: TQ 198058.

*Above: Located on the north-west corner of the airfield at Shoreham Airport, this Anti-aircraft dome trainer is one of number of surviving wartime buildings on the airfield. As indicated this dome trainer was used to train air and ground gunners. Films of attacking aircraft were projected on the curved ceiling with sound effects. When the guns were fired points of light appeared on the film with the accuracy estimated by the instructor, (Photographed with the kind assistance of Mr D.F. Mace).*

It was in late 1939 that the inventor Henry Stephen    came up with the idea of using films to train anti-aircraft gunners - whilst watching a newsreel in a cinema!. Following further research it was decided to build these domes, from 1941 onwards, with a radius of 10 to 20 foot. The actual image of the aircraft was projected onto the projection surface by the use of 16mm or 35mm projection equipment. Further reality was provided by the use of fluorescent light which flooded the whole area with blue light, creating the illusion of a cloudless sky.

The trainee gunner used dummy guns, which were fitted with a small projector which shone a spot of light at the point where the trainee was firing. and this enabled the instructor to make an estimation of accuracy. On pulling the trigger, a soundtrack produced the sound of a firing gun - but this would only last continuously for about 5 seconds, this being the time it took to empty the ammunition cartridge.

> Access: By foot along public footpath south from the end of Ham Lane.
> Map reference: SZ 834949.

*Above: These rusting steel struts are all that remains of a British Army bailey bridge that was placed across the Broad Rife on Selsey Bill, which can be reached by foot along a footpath from Ham Road. Unfortunately with the passage of time the bridge has collapsed and fallen into the Broad Rife - only a very brave person would use it now to cross the river!.*

The bailey bridge was one of those inventions that was to prove invaluable to the British Army once it went onto the offensive. The ease of transport and construction of these bridges ensured that the British Army was able to cross rivers where the bridges had been blown up quickly, and therefore lose little momentum in an advance. Indeed this was to be the case after D-Day in the advances across France and Germany.

This bridge was almost certainly placed across the Broad Rife near Selsey Bill some time after 1942. By this time the risk of a German invasion was minimal, and the training of the British and Canadian troops in the area increasing daily. Built by the engineers from either the British or Canadian armies, providing them with valuable experience, the bridge would then have enabled infantry and armoured units to train and exercise on the beaches and flood plains of this part of Selsey Bill.

# CHICHESTER
## A 'COLONY' OF AIR RAID SHELTERS

Access: By foot in the grounds of Chichester High School for Boys.
Map reference: SU 864042.

*Left: A view of the four 50 person shelters that can still seen today in a line within the grounds of the Chichester High School for Boys. All the structures are in good condition, though the doorways have all been bricked up using 'breeze blocks'. An interesting feature that has not been found on any other similar shelters in Sussex are that a couple of the structures have ventilation stacks fitted to the roofs, (Photographed by the kind permission of the Headmaster of the Chichester High School for Boys).*

It is unusual to find so many of these '50 person shelters' located in one place like this within Sussex. As the German aerial bombardment of many of Britain's bigger towns and cities intensified, 'colonies' of these types of shelter did begin to appear. Commonly located on the outskirts of large urban areas, these 'colonies' could consist of as many as 15 of these shelters all in one group. Built by the local authority these shelters were intended to house those people who would flee from the city at night in the hope of avoiding the devastating air attacks that might have been going on at the time. This small 'colony' might well have been built in the school grounds by virtue of the fact that Chichester was a frequent target - a legacy of the nearby railway line, station and goods yard.

# PEACEHAVEN
## LIGHT ANTI-AIRCRAFT GUN EMPLACEMENTS

*Access: By foot along track south from The Highway.*
*Map reference: TQ 431005.*

*Above: One of two remaining light anti-aircraft gun emplacements that can be found on the coast near Peacehaven. It is known that the other emplacements that once formed a considerable concentration of light anti-aircraft guns were demolished to make way for a caravan park to the right-hand side of this picture. In this picture can be seen the main features of such an emplacement - in the foreground is the concrete wall that surrounds the gun floor, whilst at the rear is the ammunition locker and shelter - both of concrete and steel construction.*

This emplacement was built to house either a 40mm Bofors light anti-aircraft gun, or the slightly heavier 3.7 inch anti-aircraft gun. The latter was, according to the wartime handbook of the British Army, the standard equipment of the mobile (and sometimes fixed) anti-aircraft batteries used in home defence. The manual goes on to state that a considerable number of these guns were emplaced on concrete platforms. It is therefore likely that the 3.7 inch weapon was used here at Peacehaven. It fired a 28-pound high explosive projectile upto a maximum height of some 30,000 feet.

The emplacements shown here were unusual in that they were more permanent than most light anti-aircraft sites - a brick wall replacing the earth bank around the gun floor, and a more substantial concrete and steel shelter present. The shelter would have been used for the location for maintenance on the gun, as well as providing a storage and rest area for the actual gun crews.

*Above: A view of the inside of the main shelter, where much of the original paint can be seen on the walls. This area would have been where the crews not only carried out maintenance on the gun, but would have rested and sheltered in between alerts or drills. Below: Another view of the shelter. The rear part has been built from corrugated steel sheets, whilst the front section from steel reinforced concrete blocks. In the background is the concrete wall that lined the gun floor.*

# SHOREHAM-BY-SEA
## HARBOUR SEARCH LIGHT TOWER

> Access: By foot along path from old Coastguard Station, Fort Haven.
> Map reference: TQ 235045.

*Right: Standing on the western side of the harbour entrance at Shoreham Port is this brick searchlight tower. Entrance is made through a doorway at the rear, though the wooden board on the front has been added later. Also at the rear is a small store room area which would have been used possibly for the storage of spares for the searchlight or for communication equipment.*

Almost all of the ports and harbours of the UK were equipped with searchlight facilities soon after the beginning of the Second World War. These searchlights would have been housed in variety of structures, ranging from simple pits, through to searchlight towers as above and even in specially designed pillboxes. Power would either have been supplied directly from the national grid (with back-up generators), or from the searchlight post's own power supply. The purpose of the searchlights were not to detect enemy aircraft, but primarily in the detection of enemy ships - such as the fast surface E-boats or even surfaced submarines. Once caught in the beam of the searchlight, which sometimes were directed by radar, the vessel would then come under fire from the surrounding coastal artillery.

# POLING
## RADAR STATION DEFENCES

Access: By foot along public footpath from the end of Poling Street.
Map reference: TQ 041047.

*Left: Hidden in the undergrowth is this pillbox, which appears to have been constructed from the Type 22 plans drawn up at the beginning of the war by the Directorate of Fortifications, then a part of the war office. Hidden by the tree on the left is one of the three embrasures that would have been used to fire the light machine gun through - this being basically an anti-infantry pillbox. The entrance is located on the north-west corner and is protected by a blast wall.*

Located so near the coast, the threat of a land attack on the radar station at Poling was very real, as was the case at many of the other radar stations such as at Pevensey, (see page 23). As a result an integral part of the radar site was its defences, which would have consisted of a number of pillboxes, infantry slit trenches and even mortar posts.

The pillbox shown here can be found south from the original radar site adjacent to a public footpath that heads south from the end of Poling Street. Local rumour has it that this pillbox could once be reached via a tunnel that led from the radar site, though this is more likely to have been the tunnel that was known to have led from the radar site to its buried reserve also south from the where the masts once stood.

# EAST LAVANT
## UNDERGROUND AIRFIELD SHELTER

Location: In the grounds of a private residence off the Lavant Straight.
Map reference: SU 866079.

*Above: One of the many surviving structures from the wartime airfield at Westhampnett is this underground air-raid shelter. The front entrance, (above), has been photographed by the author whilst standing on some of the old concrete access roads that were laid throughout this part of East Lavant. The airfield itself is some way to the south of this private garden, , (Photographed with the kind permission of Mr E. Lewis-Bowen).*

This brick and concrete shelter is of a design common to many British airfields, and is roughly similar to the standard '50 person shelter' that can be found described elsewhere in this book. Entrance is made down brick steps located at each end of the structure, though on opposite sides. Being  partly or completely buried, the roof of the shelter would then be covered with an earth bank - as is the case here. The size of the structure is roughly 35ft x 10ft x 7ft high.

Despite the fact that this shelter is located in a private garden, there is plenty of evidence to suggest that this was once a busy area of the airfields out-sites.  In surrounding gardens can be found Nissen Huts, further evidence of concrete road-ways, air ministry water towers and even washrooms!. The current owner of the land states that his house was built in 1960 replacing these Nissen Huts, and says that local rumours tell the story that Douglas Bader once was billeted in the Nissen huts that surrounded this shelter. He also believes that as the risk of air attack reduced, the shelter was used to store ammunition.

*Above: The inside of the shelter, with the main entrance in the background. Whilst taking these photographs, the author found further evidence of the shelters wartime use in a 1937 pattern British Army water-bottle hidden in a dark corner!. Note the new resident clinging to the roof. Left: Another view of the main entrance steps, included to show one important feature - the drain. This was included to remove the risk of the shelter being flooded. The floor at the two entrances is sloped towards the drains. (Photographs taken with the kind permission of Mr E. Lewis-Bowen).*

> Access: By foot along the cliff top path east from Newhaven Fort.
> Map reference: TQ 447001.

*Right: The ramps and steps that lead up past the stores and offices to the gun floor on the cliff top at Newhaven, west from the Fort itself. There are in fact three of these batteries located adjacent to each other on the cliff-top, all being of identical design. The buildings on the left of the picture would have included the cartridge store, a shell store, rest room, and even an office for the battery commander.*

The layout of these batteries indicates that whilst certainly in use during the Second World War, as indicated by graffiti located within some of the buildings, they were built towards the beginning of the 20th Century. The fact that there are three of these batteries in a row, each consisting of a single heavy open concrete emplacement surrounded by ammunition lockers and with the associated buildings behind and below the gun-floor supports this view. It is therefore likely that these batteries were built at about the time of the First World War to house 9.2 inch guns intended to fire upon German shipping in the Channel. They were in use throughout the Second World War, controlled by the battery observation posts and radar equipment located at nearby Newhaven Fort.

*Above: A view of the gun floor itself, with the location of the gun mount indicated by a somewhat hardy shrub!. Located around the gun floor and in the rear of the surrounding buildings are the ammunition lockers and cartridge stores. In the background can be seen the English Channel where, guided by the radar and battery observation posts at Newhaven Fort, the gun of this battery would have fired upon any approaching German naval vessel. Left: One of the various store buildings located further down the hillside behind the gun floor - possibly the shell or cartridge store.*

Access: By foot in Holtye Avenue at the junction with Quarry Rise.
Map reference: TQ 402395.

*Left: A pub sign with a difference. The Guinea-pig with wings, flames and crashing aircraft are all clues to the reason behind the name of this pub, being named after the 'Guinea-Pig Club' which was founded in 1941.*

The Guinea-Pig Public House was named after the famous Guinea-Pig Club, which was founded in 1941 for serving airforce personnel of all nations who had been treated at the nearby Queen Victoria by Sir Archibald McIndoe.

McIndoe was born in 1900 at Dunedin, New Zealand. Having qualified, he moved to London in 1930 and worked under Sir Harold Gillies, a plastic surgeon. In 1939, McIndoe moved to East Grinstead, where, at the Queen Victoria Hospital, he set up his own burns unit. At the time, treatment of burns usually involved tannic acid or animal fat, but McIndoe pioneered the replacement of skin and rebuilding of faces and limbs. Many an airman injured in aerial combat passed through East Grinstead, and so it was that they formed themselves into the Guinea-Pig club, of which McIndoe was the first president.

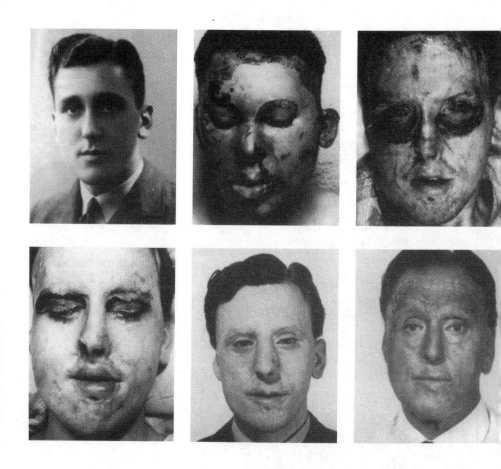

*Above: This fascinating series of photographs show the work of the Burns Unit at the Queen Victor Hospital at East Grinstead. The person shown would have been eligible for membership of the Guine pig club, being a fighter pilot badly burnt whilst trying to escape from his aircraft. Once at the Que Victoria Hospital, the techniques pioneered by Sir Archibald McIndoe would have been used on again on this person. The 6 photographs show the pilot before receiving his injuries, through t initial injuries, treatment and then final success. (Photographs reproduced by the kind permission the Trustees and staff of the Queen Victoria Hospital NHS Trust).*

*Access: By foot in Churchyard of Climping Church, Church Lane.*
*Map reference: TQ 003027.*

*Above and below: On the 18th August 1940, at the height of the Battle of Britain, the naval air-station at Ford was heavily bombed by the German airforce. Police records show that an unknown number of high explosive bombs were dropped, with 39 people killed and 2 injured. The picture below shows the memorial that was erected in 1942 in Climping Churchyard. It is interesting in that the barbed wire perimeter can be seen in the background, (Photograph by kind permission of Mr A. Saunders).*

# APPEAL FOR INFORMATION

The author would be interested to learn of any wreck, relic or memorial that remains in East or West Sussex from either of the two World Wars. Such a site could include any of the following:
-Pillboxes, bunkers and emplacements;
- Air raid shelters whether surface or buried, and including those in the grounds of private dwellings;
- Anti-aircraft gun sites, ammunition stores, target ranges and even shell craters;
- Remains of any military, RAF, Naval, P.O.W. or refugee camps;
- Graves, memorials, plagues and statues;
- Vehicle, boat or aircraft remains.
If you have any information and/or photographs (old or new) on anything that might fit in the realms of this book or the above list, please write to the following address. Even if the subject has been demolished or no longer remains, the author would still very much like to hear. If writing please include as much location detail as possible.

Martin F. Mace,
Historic Military Press,
Green Arbor,
Rectory Road,
Storrington,
West Sussex, RH20 4ES.

# ACKNOWLEDGEMENTS

As with all research projects of this size there is always a large number of people who deserve thanks. In particular I need to thank my girlfriend Tracey, who, whatever the weather (or thickness of mud!), visited the majority of the sites listed here, and was always ready to listen and offer seemingly endless help and advice. Just as importantly, it was Tracey who did her utmost to ensure that the deadlines set for this book were adhered to!. This book is dedicated to Tracey's perseverance. I must also thank my mother and father, Peter and Anne-Marie Mace, for their support and encouragement, and Barry and Wendy Dickens from BDA Associates who have ensured that this book was able to be printed and or always having the time to answer my questions.

Finding all these sites was no mean task, but two people in particular have provided much valuable help. Andy Oliver not only spent time finding some of the sites, but helped in providing photographs and background information. Michael Boulton also dipped into his mountain of knowledge, and brought to my attention a number of the sites - especially in the Newhaven areas. Other locations were found after the kind help of Dr. Mike Osborne (Defence of Britain Project); Glen Bruce; Paul Motte-Harrison and Joan Ham (a historian on the Storrington and Sullington area).

Having located a site, background research was often required, and in this respect the following people are owed my thanks: Margaret Courtney (Guides Association); Shelly Woodroffe (Royal National Lifeboats Institution); Alan Readman (West Sussex County Records Office); Mrs S. Berry (Arun District Council); Mr G.D. Rudram and Peter Stainthorpe (Commonwealth War Graves Commission).

A number of the sites within this book are located on private property. The following persons kindly took the time to listen to my requests and allow me permission to enter their land or arranging permission to do so: Mr David Langmead; Mr Keith Langmead; Mr E. Lewis-Owen; Mrs C. Mates; The Landlord of the Dragon Inn Public House, Colegate; Mrs Sara Rodger (Arundel Castle); Mr Andrew James (Dorset House); The Director Wiston House; The Staff and Director of Newhaven Fort and Ms Allex Jenkinson and Mr Jim Tweed of the Sussex Archaeological Society.

# PICTURE SOURCES

Lastly I must pass onto the area of photographs. The illustrations in this book have in most cases been amassed over the years by the author, and so, unless stated, the pictures are sourced from the authors collection. Some, however, have been provided by other people or collections and I also gratefully thank these people:

Page s 56, 119, 143, 162 and 187. These wartime pictures are all produced by kind permission of Mr Andy Saunders, and come from his excellent series of books on the wartime Sussex aircraft crash sites. The picture on page 132 comes from Andy Saunders book 'Bognor at War', and is also produced with his kind permission.
Pages 63, 106 and 124. These wartime pictures are produced by kind permission of Mrs Mary Taylor, and come from her books 'Rustington at War' and Littlehampton in the War Years'.
Pages 116 and 164. These wartime R.O.C. photographs come from the book 'Attack Warning Red', and are produced here by the kind permission of Mr Derek Wood.
Page 133. This photograph is reproduced by the kind permission of Dr. Mike Osborne.
Page 137. Reproduced by kind permission of Mrs J. Knight and the Director of the West Sussex County Times.
Page 142. This unique picture comes from the book 'Dive Sussex', the permission kindly given by its author Mr Kendall Macdonald.
Page 9. The illustration on this page is reproduced from an original on Page 20, July 1986 issue of FlyPast Magazine by the kind permission of the Editor, Mr Ken Delve.
Page 37. Produced from an original in 'Storrington in Living Memory', by kind permission of Joan Ham.
Page 89. By kind permission of Kevin Gordon, Mrs Pat Berry and Directors of Seaford Museum.
Page 92. Submarine E-46 (ref 4434) and page 93 L/Commander Naper (ref 7811) are produced by the kind permission of the Royal Navy Submarine Museum, Gosport, Hants.
Page 17 is produced by kind permission of Dee Leighton.
Page 158 contains a drawing reproduced by permission of Mr Glen Bruce.
Page 158. The wartime photograph (ref 2805/A1) is produced by kind permission of Mr D. Fletcher and the Director of the Tank Museum, Bovington, Dorset.
Page 165. By kind permission of Mr J.A.A. Bernier.

Permission to photograph the displays in Fort Newhaven, (pages 83 and 117) was kindly given by the Director of Fort Newhaven. The wall art at Michelham Priory was photographed by permission of the Sussex Archaeological Society. The mural at Wiston was photographed by permission of the Director of Wiston House. The Pickett-Hamilton Fort at Tangmere was photographed by kind permission of the Curator of Tangmere Military Aviation Museum. I would also like to thank my Grandfather, Denis Mace, who also travelled to some of the sites to assist in photographing the less accessible remains.

A great many people have assisted in some way or other in this project - and to everyone pass my grateful thanks: